Victorian Woodturnings and Woodwork

Victorian Woodturnings and Woodwork

BLUMER & KUHN STAIR CO.

DOVER PUBLICATIONS, INC.
Mineola, New York

Bibliographical Note

This Dover edition, first published in 2006, contains a facsimile of the Blumer & Kuhn Stair Co. catalog of Stairs, Stair Railing, Balusters, Newel Posts, Mantels, Pew Ends, etc., originally published by Rand, McNally & Company, Chicago, in 1893.

Library of Congress Cataloging-in-Publication Data

Victorian woodturnings and woodwork / Blumer & Kuhn Stair Co.
     p. cm.
  Reprint. originally published: Chicago : Rand, McNally, 1893.
  ISBN-13: 978-0-486-45114-5
  ISBN-10: 0-486-45114-3 (pbk.)
  1. Millwork (Woodwork)—Catalogs. 2. Blumer and Kuhn (Firm)—Catalogs. 3. Architectural woodwork—Catalogs. 4. Architecture, Victorian. I. Blumer and Kuhn (Firm).

TS853.V53 2006
721'.0448—dc22

                                   2006045446

www.doverpublications.com

Blumer & Kuhn Stair Co.

WHOLESALE MANUFACTURERS OF

STAIRS, STAIR RAILING,

Balusters, Newel Posts, Mantels

Pew Ends, Etc.

ALSO

INTERIOR FINISH

Of every description in all kinds of Hard and Soft Woods

Brackets, Corner and Plinth Blocks,

TURNED PORCH ⚬ VERANDA WORK, ETC.

ST. LOUIS, MO.

CHICAGO:
PUBLISHED BY RAND, McNALLY & COMPANY,
Printers, Engravers, and Electrotypers.
1893.

[Original title page]

INDEX.

E. W. BLUMER, President.   HENRY KUHN, Sec'y & Treas.

Office of
Blumer & Kuhn Stair Co.
MANUFACTURERS OF
BALUSTERS, RAILING
❄ **NEWEL POSTS,**
AND ALL KINDS OF STAIR MATERIAL.
Dock Street and Broadway.

To the Trade.

St. LOUIS, Mo., May 1, 1893.

Dear Sir:

We take great pleasure in presenting you herewith a copy of our new price list, together with designs for Stair Work, Turned Porch and Veranda Work, Brackets, Corner and Plinth Blocks, Mantels, Church Pews, Mouldings of any design, and especially do we ask you to examine our latest designs for Stair Newel Posts as designated on page 14.

In order to meet the large and increasing demand for our specialties, we were compelled to increase our facilities by the addition of a large and modern Branch Factory, with all the latest and most approved machinery adapted to the different parts of the work. These additional facilities together with the Parent Factory, will enable us to meet all demands made upon us promptly and in a more satisfactory manner, both to ourselves and our clients than heretofore.

Our stock on hand is at all times large and of the choicest grades, being thoroughly air-dried, which, with our ample facilities for kiln-drying, enables us to furnish work that we can guarantee to be satisfactory, being executed by competent and skilled workmen, of which we employ only the best.

We shall be pleased to receive your orders for anything in our line, and will cheerfully quote you prices on memoranda or details for any of the above class of work.

Inviting a personal inspection of our stock, and hoping to receive your orders, we are

Yours truly,

Blumer & Kuhn Stair Co.

STAIR PLANS.

Stairs, Newel Posts
✳ Balusters
Stair Railing.

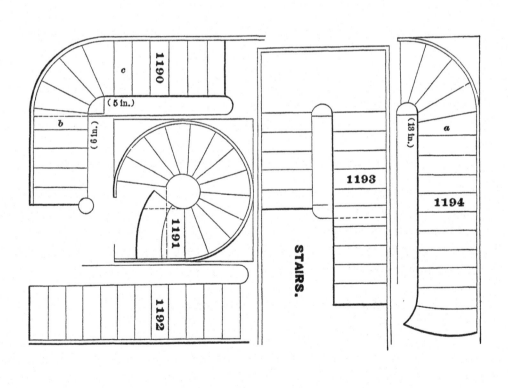

STAIRS, NEWEL POSTS, BALUSTERS, STAIR RAILING, ETC.

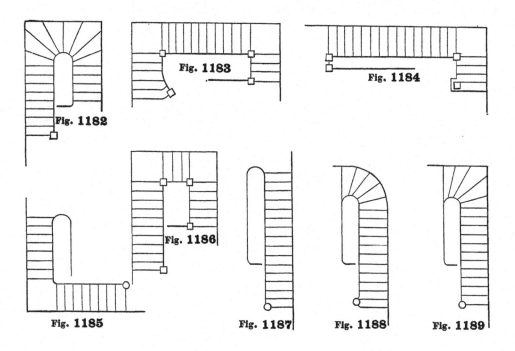

Fig. 1182   Fig. 1183   Fig. 1184

Fig. 1185   Fig. 1186   Fig. 1187   Fig. 1188   Fig. 1189

DIRECTIONS NECESSARY FOR ORDERING STAIRS AND STAIR RAILING.

When a flight of stairs is wanted, we should know the height of story from floor to floor, width of joists in second story, width and run of stairs, the size of cylinder, style of base used in the hall, with rough sketch showing about the shape of stairs wanted.

FOR STAIR RAILING, STRAIGHT FLIGHT,

We require the width of rise and step as sawed out on string board, the number of risers, the size of cylinder from face to face of string or face board, which way it turns at head of stairs, and the number of feet of straight rail required at landing. Unless we receive plan showing otherwise, we always suppose the top riser for a straight flight of stairs to be placed at the edge or spring of cylinder.

FOR CIRCULAR OR WINDING STAIRS,

We should have an exact plan of stairs as built, giving the width of rise and step, the location of risers in cylinder, etc.; and, when there are straight steps below or above the cylinder, always give the distance from the first square riser to the edge or spring line of cylinder, on the face of string or face board. *Always write your address in full on the plans.*

PRICE LIST OF STAIR WORK.

LIBERAL DISCOUNT TO DEALERS.

BALUSTERS.

We turn all our Stair Balusters 2 ft. 4 in. and 2 ft. 8 in. long, unless otherwise ordered. Are prepared to furnish, on short notice, any length or style desired. Odd lengths cost extra.

Fancy Turned Balusters.
Nos. 1200 and 1201.

Sizes.	1½ in.	1¾ in.	2 in.	2¼ in.	2½ in.
	Cts.	Cts.	Cts.	Cts.	Cts.
Oak or Ash...	9	12	12	15	17
Wal't or Ch'ry,	11	17	17	21	23

Nos. 1202 and 1203.

S'zes.	1½ in.	1¾ in.	2 in.	2¼ in.	2½ in.
	Cts.	Cts.	Cts.	Cts.	Cts.
Oak or Ash....	11	14	14	17	19
Wal't or Ch'ry.	13	19	19	23	25

Nos. 1206 to 1214 inclusive.

Sizes.	1¾ in.	2 in.	2¼ in.	2½ in.	2¾ in.
	Cts.	Cts.	Cts.	Cts.	Cts.
Oak or Ash....	17	17	20	22	30
Wal't or Ch'ry.	22	22	26	29	43

Octagon Balusters.
No. 1205.

Sizes.	1¾ in.	2 in.	2¼ in.	2½ in.	2¾ in.
	Cts.	Cts.	Cts.	Cts.	Cts.
Oak or Ash....	19	19	23	25	35
Wal't or Ch'ry.	24	24	29	31	48

For No. 1204, Fluted, add to list of No. 1205 1c. Mahogany costs about double price.

NEWELS.
Fancy Turned Newel Posts.
Nos. 1300 and 1301.

Sizes.	4 in.	5 in.	6 in.	7 in.
Pine..................	$ .90	$1.25	$1.50	
Oak or Ash............	3.00	3.50	4.00	$4.50
Walnut or Cherry......	3.50	4.00	4.50	5.00

Plain Octagon Staved Newel Posts.
No. 1802, Walnut, Cherry, Oak, or Ash.

Sizes.	8 in.	9 in.	10 in.	11 in.	12 in.
Prices.	$5.75	$6.00	$6.25	$6.50	$7.00

For Raised O G Panels, add to above prices $1.50 each.
For Mahogany Posts, add to above prices $4.00 each.

Octagon Sunk Panel Newel Posts.
FANCY MOULDED.
No. 1303, Walnut, Cherry, Oak, or Ash.

Sizes.	8 in.	9 in.	10 in.	11 in.	12 in.
Prices.	$8.50	$9.00	$9.50	$10.00	$10.50

For Circle Top Panels, add $1.25
For Posts like No. 1304, add $3.00
For Posts like No. 1305, add $4.50

PLATFORM OR ANGLE NEWELS.

Sizes.	Oak or Ash.	Walnut or Cherry.
No. 1501, 5 inch.........	$4.50	$5.00
No. 1502, 5 inch.........	5.00	5.50
No. 1503, 5 inch.........	6.50	7.00
No. 1504, 5 inch.........	5.00	5.50
No. 1505, 5 inch.........	6.50	7.00
No. 1506, 5 inch.........	7.00	7.50

POSTS FOR OUTSIDE BALUSTRADE.

Pine, ordinary lengths (see page 44).

Numbers.	Price, 3¾ inches.	Price, 4¾ inches.	Price, 5¾ inches.
1630	$ .75	$1.00	$1.25
1631	.75	1.00	1.25
1632	1.00	1.25	1.50
1634	1.50	1.75	2.00
1635		1.75	2.00
1639	2.00	2.25	2.50
1640	1.00	1.25	1.50

TURNED BALUSTERS.

For Outside Balustrade see pages 45 and 49.

Prices in Pine or Whitewood.

Length, inches.	8	10	12	14	16	18	20	22	24
	Cts.	Cts.	Cts.	Cts.	Cts.	Cts.	Cts.	Cts.	Cts.
Size, 1¾ x 1¾ in.	6	6	6	7	8	9	11		
Size, 2¾ x 2¾ in.		8	9	10	11	12	13		
Size, 3¾ x 3¾ in.		12	13	14	15	16	17	19	21

SAWED PINE BALUSTERS.

For any of the Patterns on pages 49 and 50, size 5¾ x ⅞ 18 or 20 inches long, price 16 cents each.

PORCH AND VERANDA COLUMNS.

Basswood or Whitewood.

4¾ to 5¾ inches square (pages 45 and 46).

Numbers.	Price, 8 ft. long.	Price, 10 ft. long.
1645	$3.00	$3.50
1646	3.00	3.50
1647	3.00	3.50
1648	3.00	3 75
1648½	4.50	5.50
1649	3.00	3 50
1650	3.00	3.50
1651	3.00	3.50
1652	3.00	3.50
1653	3.00	3.50
1654	3.00	3.50

Discounts to Dealers.

BALUSTERS.

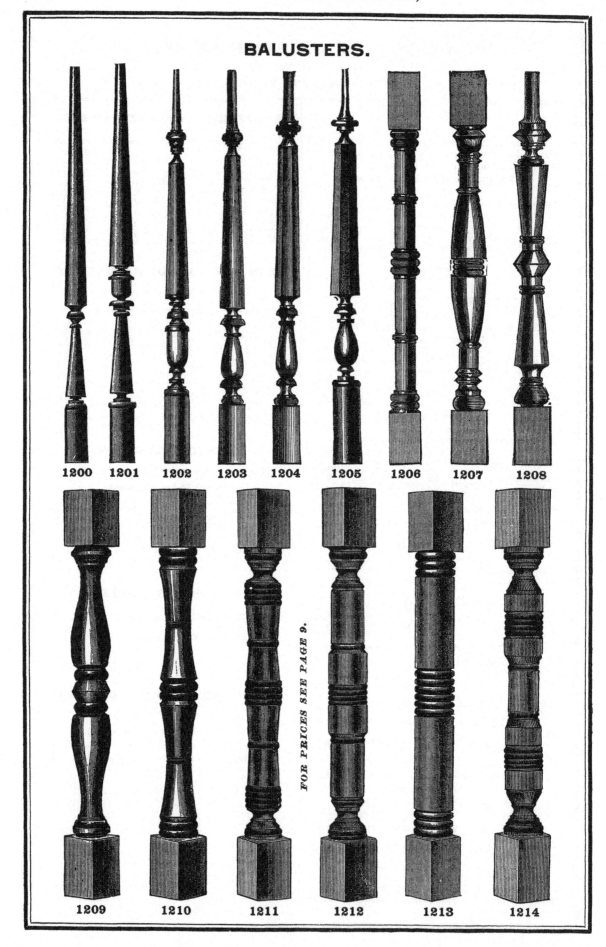

1200　　1201　　1202　　1203　　1204　　1205　　1206　　1207　　1208

FOR PRICES SEE PAGE 9.

1209　　　　1210　　　　1211　　　　1212　　　　1213　　　　1214

BALUSTERS.

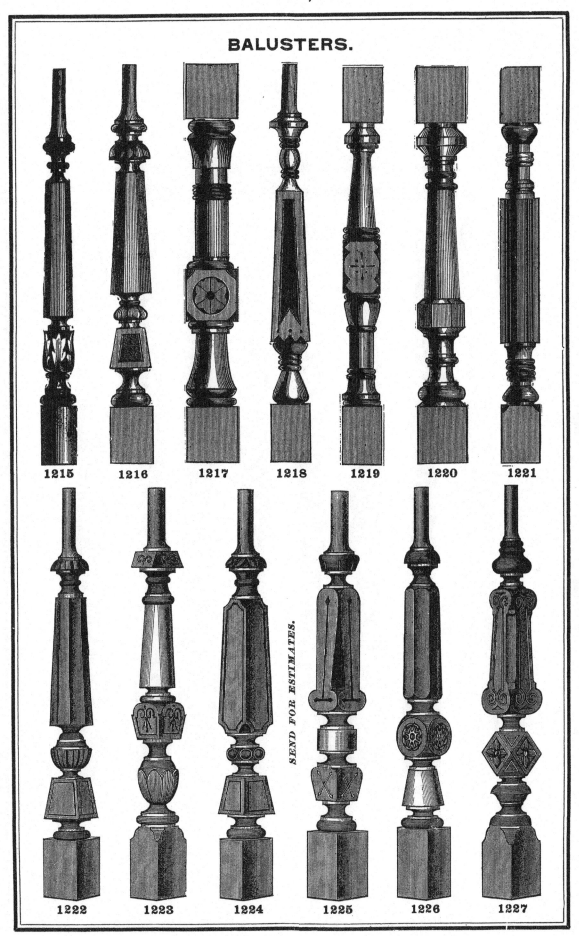

1215 1216 1217 1218 1219 1220 1221

SEND FOR ESTIMATES.

1222 1223 1224 1225 1226 1227

TWISTED BALUSTERS.

1   2   3   4   5   6   8   9

TWISTED BALUSTERS.

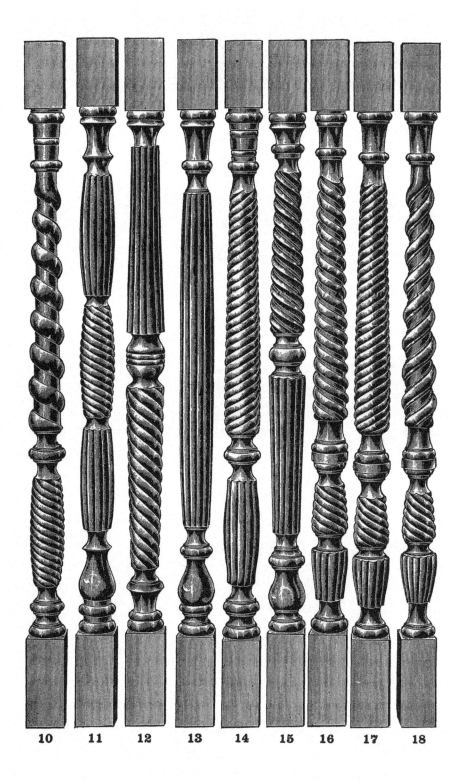

10   11   12   13   14   15   16   17   18

NEWELS.

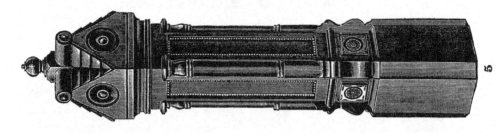

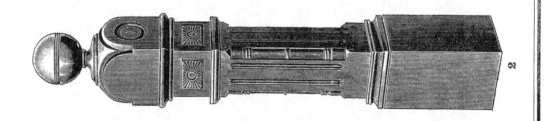

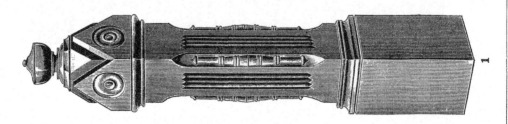

NEWEL POSTS.

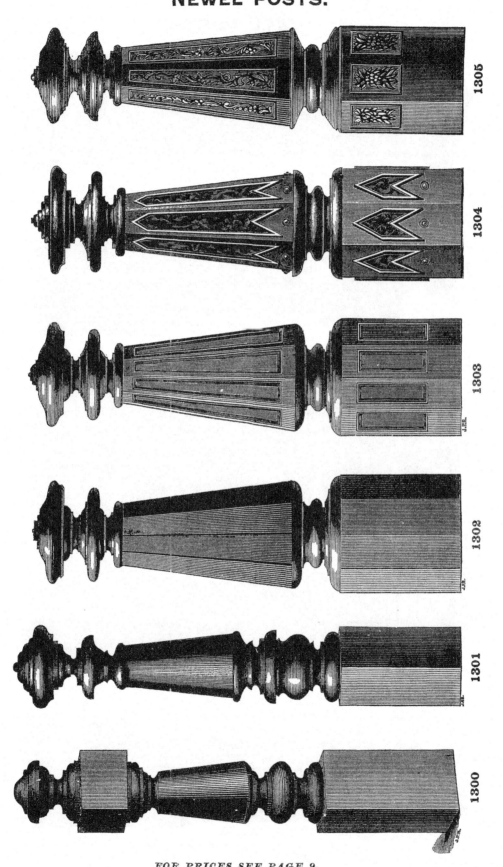

FOR PRICES SEE PAGE 9.

NEWEL POSTS.

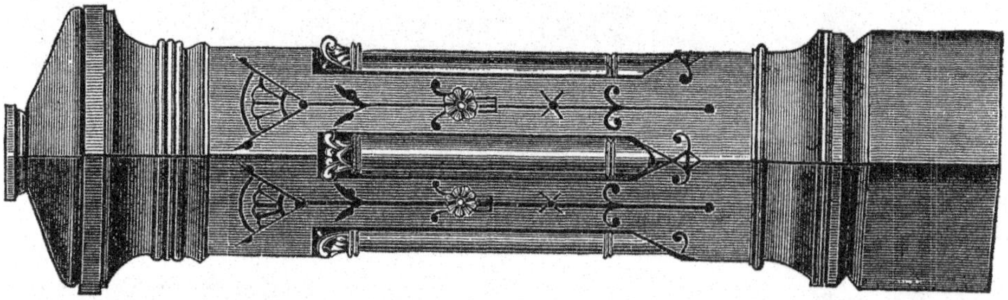

1310

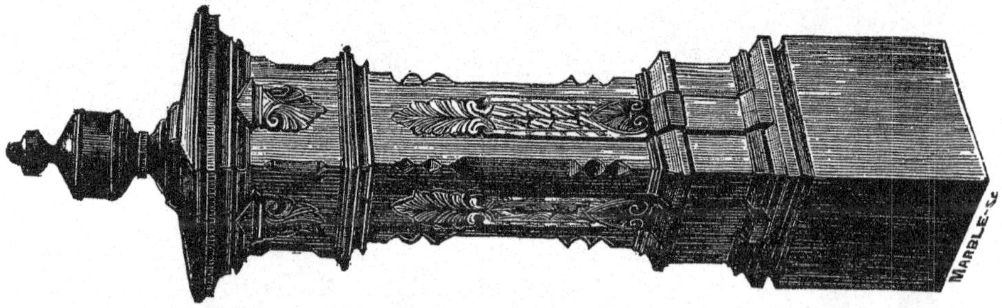

1309

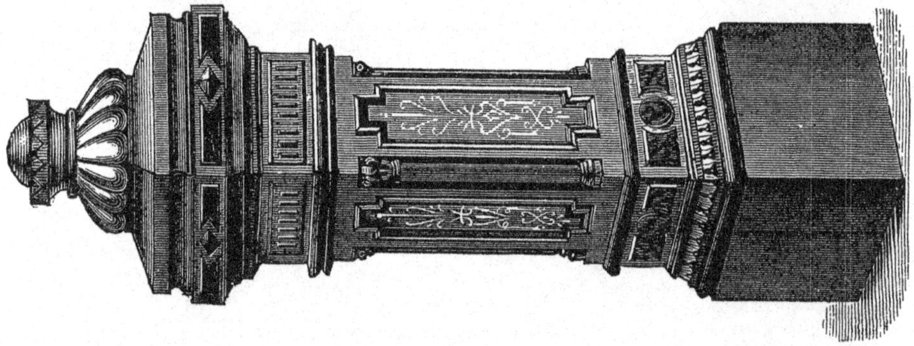

1308

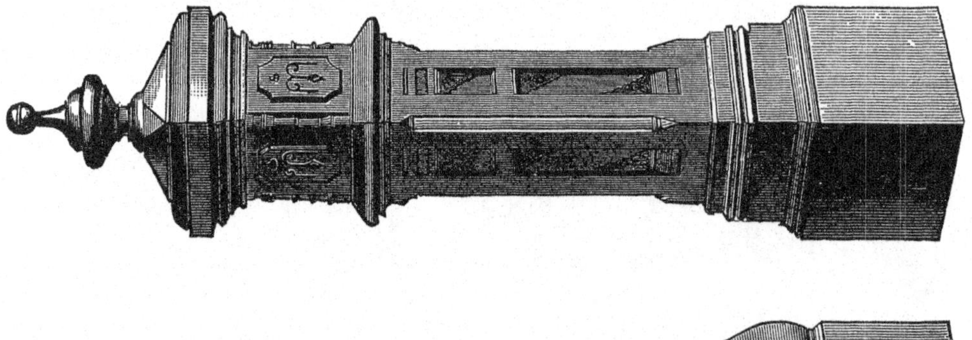

1307

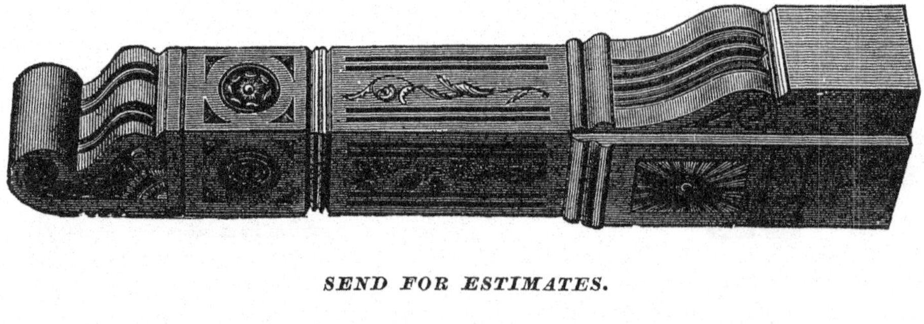

1306

SEND FOR ESTIMATES.

NEWEL POSTS.

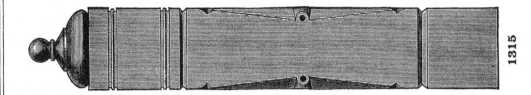

1315

1314

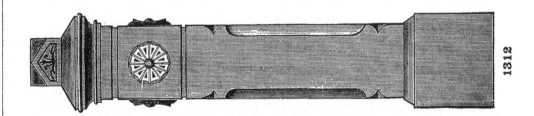

1313

1312

1311

SEND FOR ESTIMATES.

NEWEL POSTS.

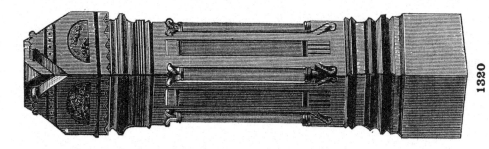

1320

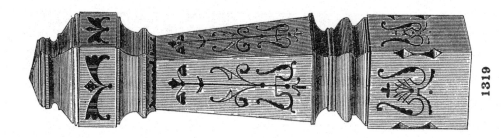

1319

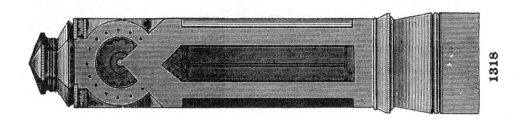

1318

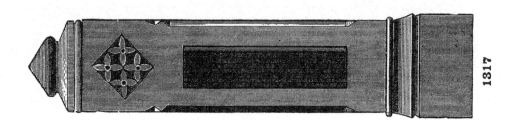

1317

1316

SEND FOR ESTIMATES.

NEWEL POSTS.

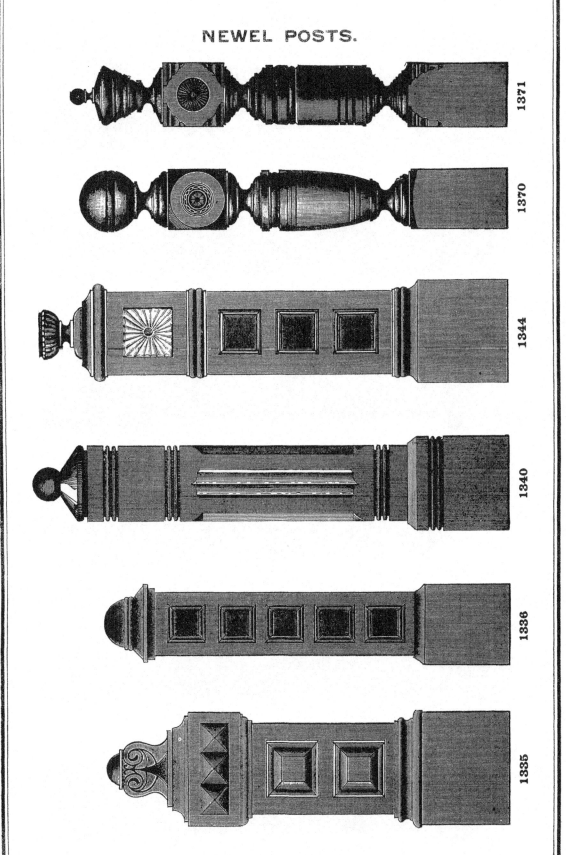

NEWELS.

1331

1330

1329

1328

1327

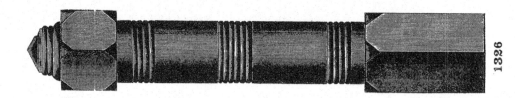

1326

WRITE FOR PRICES.

NEWELS.

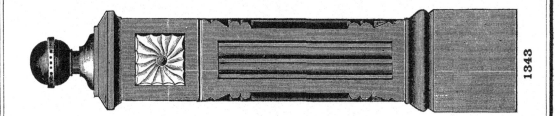

1343

1341

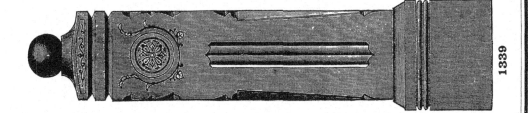

1339

STAIR RAILS.

Thickness of Rails varies from 1¾ to 2¾, proportionate to width.

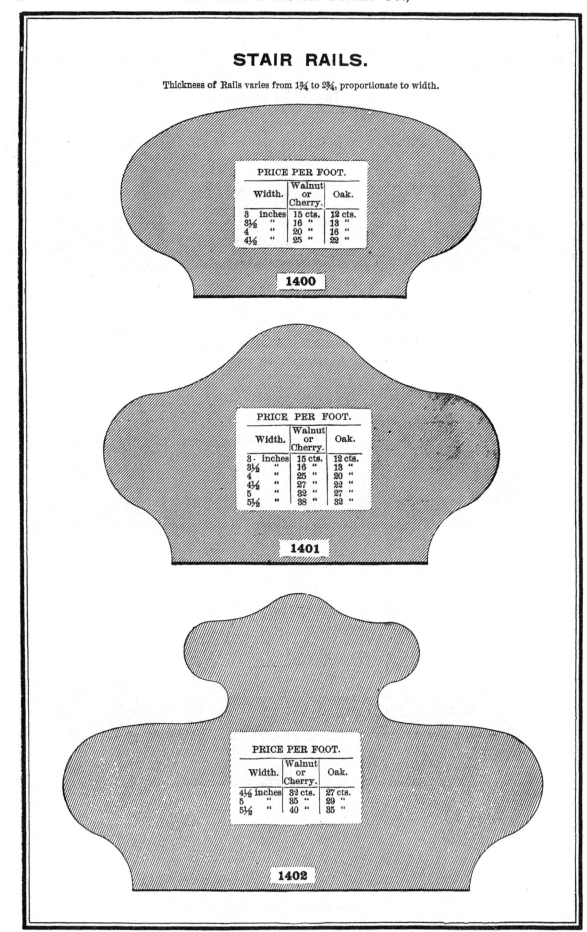

PRICE PER FOOT.

Width.	Walnut or Cherry.	Oak.
3 inches	15 cts.	12 cts.
3½ "	16 "	13 "
4 "	20 "	16 "
4½ "	25 "	22 "

1400

PRICE PER FOOT.

Width.	Walnut or Cherry.	Oak.
3 - inches	15 cts.	12 cts.
3½ "	16 "	13 "
4 "	25 "	20 "
4½ "	27 "	22 "
5 "	32 "	27 "
5½ "	38 "	32 "

1401

PRICE PER FOOT.

Width.	Walnut or Cherry.	Oak.
4½ inches	33 cts.	27 cts.
5 "	35 "	29 "
5½ "	40 "	35 "

1402

STAIR RAILS.

Thickness of Rails varies from 1¾ to 2¾, proportionate to width.

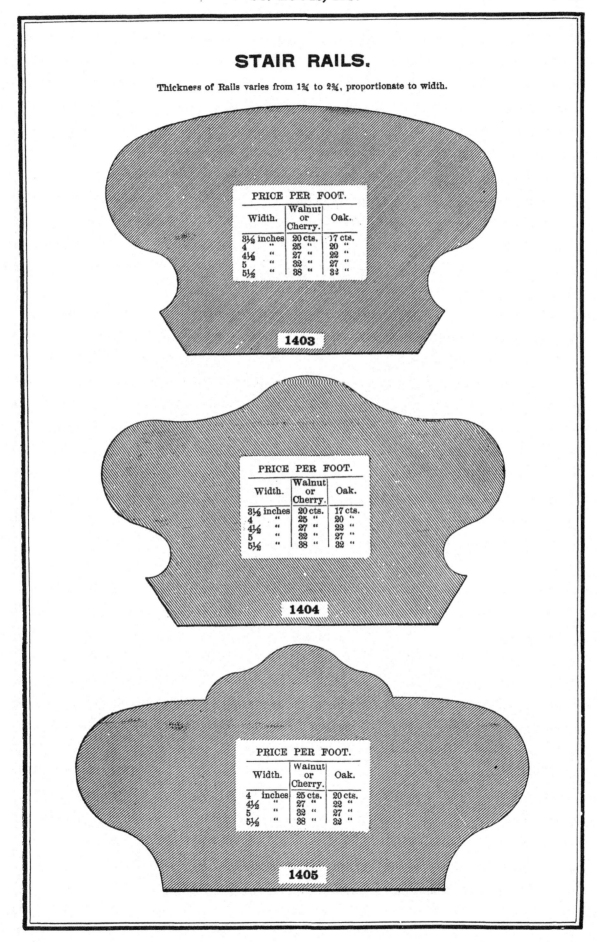

PRICE PER FOOT.

Width.	Walnut or Cherry.	Oak.
3½ inches	20 cts.	17 cts.
4 "	25 "	20 "
4½ "	27 "	22 "
5 "	32 "	27 "
5½ "	38 "	32 "

1403

PRICE PER FOOT.

Width.	Walnut or Cherry.	Oak.
3½ inches	20 cts.	17 cts.
4 "	25 "	20 "
4½ "	27 "	22 "
5 "	32 "	27 "
5½ "	38 "	32 "

1404

PRICE PER FOOT.

Width.	Walnut or Cherry.	Oak.
4 inches	25 cts.	20 cts.
4½ "	27 "	22 "
5 "	32 "	27 "
5½ "	38 "	32 "

1405

STAIR RAILS.

Thickness of Rails varies from 1¾ to 2¾, proportionate to width.

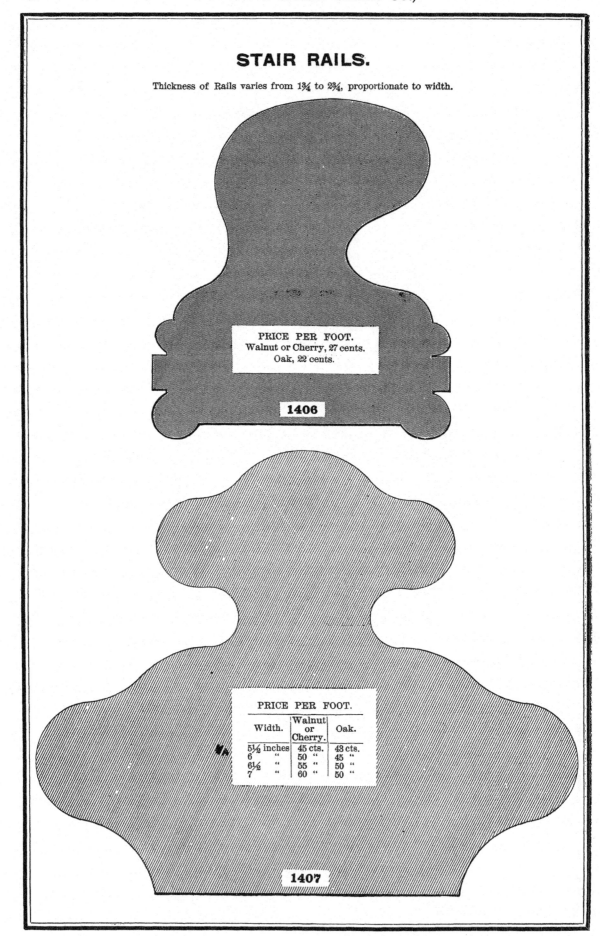

PRICE PER FOOT.
Walnut or Cherry, 27 cents.
Oak, 22 cents.

1406

PRICE PER FOOT.

Width.	Walnut or Cherry.	Oak.
5½ inches	45 cts.	43 cts.
6 "	50 "	45 "
6½ "	55 "	50 "
7 "	60 "	50 "

1407

STAIR RAILS.

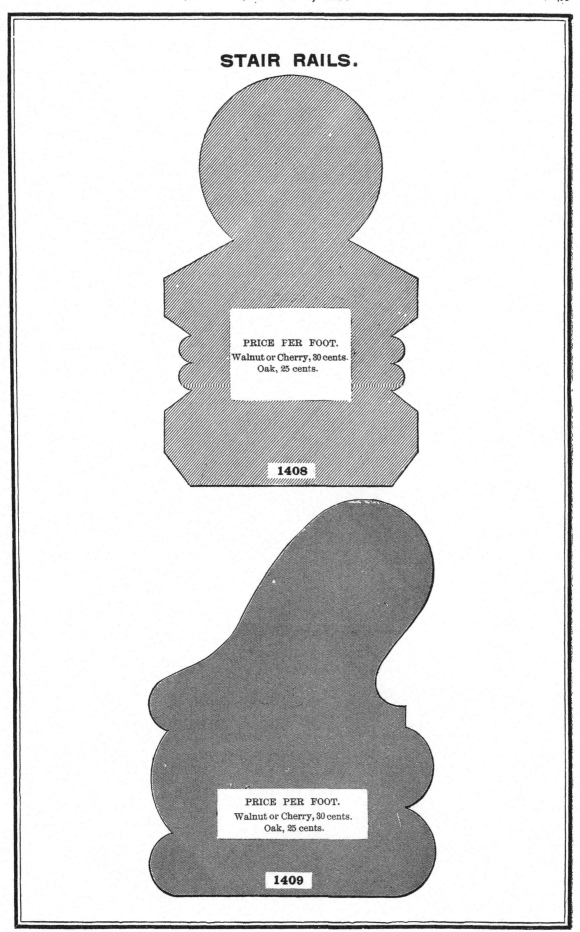

PRICE PER FOOT.
Walnut or Cherry, 30 cents.
Oak, 25 cents.

1408

PRICE PER FOOT.
Walnut or Cherry, 30 cents.
Oak, 25 cents.

1409

STAIR RAILS.

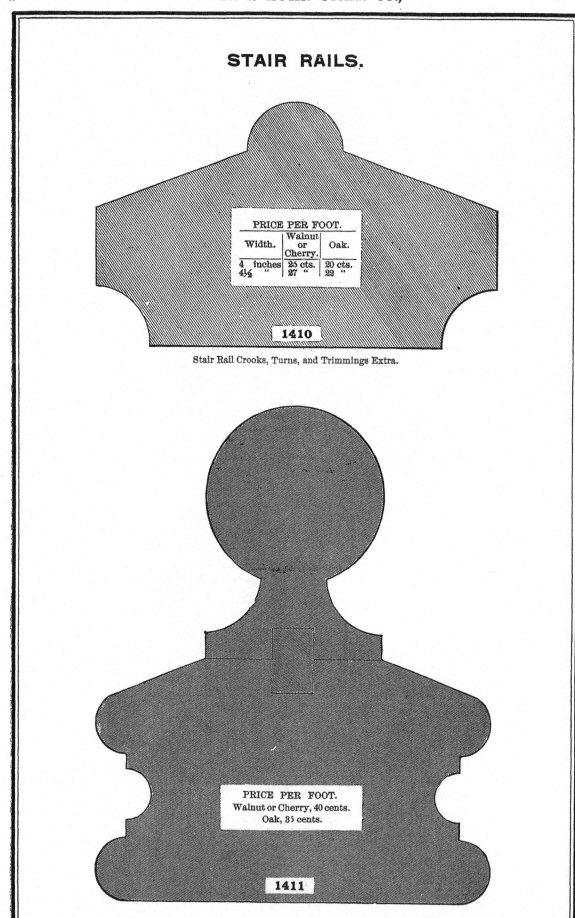

PRICE PER FOOT.

Width.	Walnut or Cherry.	Oak.
4 inches	25 cts.	20 cts.
4½ "	27 "	22 "

1410

Stair Rail Crooks, Turns, and Trimmings Extra.

PRICE PER FOOT.
Walnut or Cherry, 40 cents.
Oak, 35 cents.

1411

STAIR RAILS.

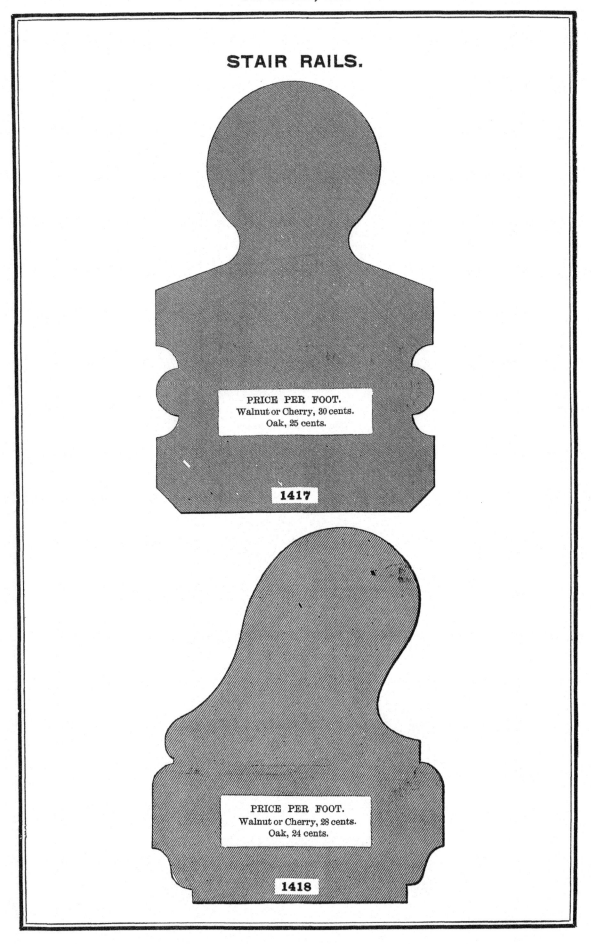

PRICE PER FOOT.
Walnut or Cherry, 30 cents.
Oak, 25 cents.

1417

PRICE PER FOOT.
Walnut or Cherry, 28 cents.
Oak, 24 cents.

1418

STAIR RAILS.

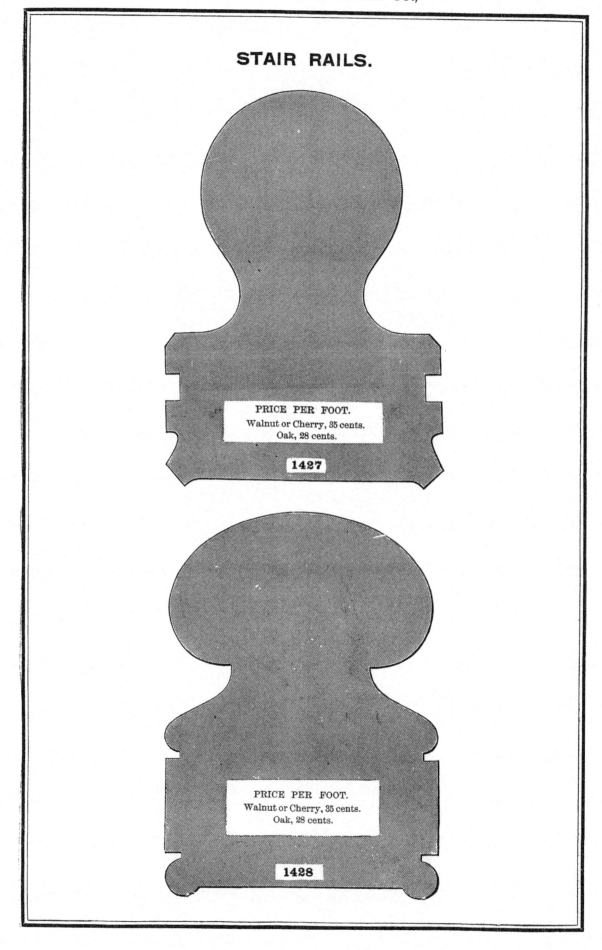

PRICE PER FOOT.
Walnut or Cherry, 35 cents.
Oak, 28 cents.

1427

PRICE PER FOOT.
Walnut or Cherry, 35 cents.
Oak, 28 cents.

1428

PLATFORM NEWELS.

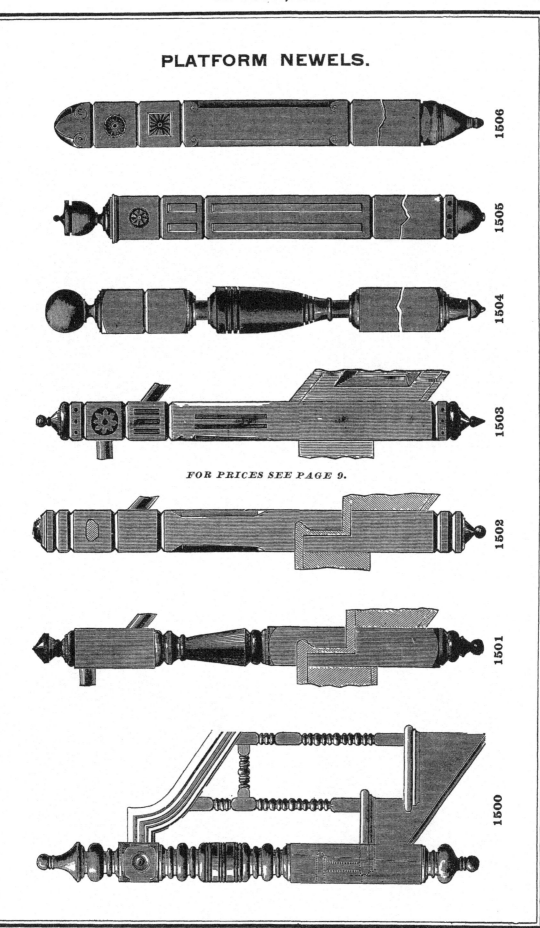

FOR PRICES SEE PAGE 9.

DESIGNS FOR STAIRS.

1520

1521

1522

1523

DESIGNS FOR STAIRS.

1524

1525

1526

1527

WRITE FOR PRICES.

DESIGN FOR STAIRS.

1528

DESIGN FOR STAIRS.

1529

DESIGN FOR STAIRS.

1530

DESIGN FOR STAIRS.

1531

DESIGN FOR STAIRS.

Balcony

1532

WRITE FOR PRICES.

DESIGNS FOR STAIRS.

1533

1534

1535

1536

WRITE FOR PRICES.

DESIGNS FOR STAIRS.

1543

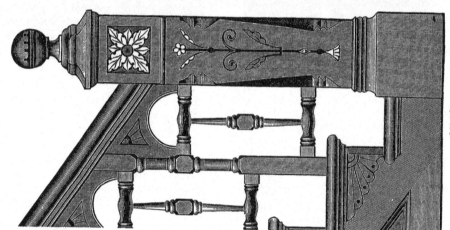

1542

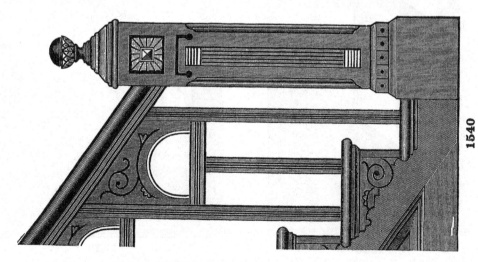

1540

DESIGNS FOR STAIRS.

1551

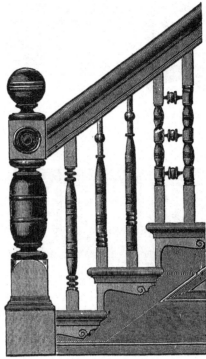

1552

1553

1554

WRITE FOR PRICES.

PORTIERE WORK.

675

Made any Size.

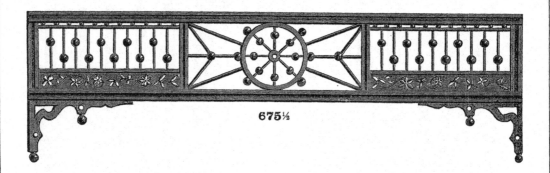

675½

676

Made any Size.

678

Portière Work of all Descriptions Made to Order.

WRITE FOR PRICES.

STAIR BRACKETS.

1575

1576

Level Brackets for Stairs, 4 inches wide. ¼ inch thick.   Price per foot: Pine, 6 cents;
Black Walnut, 10 cents.

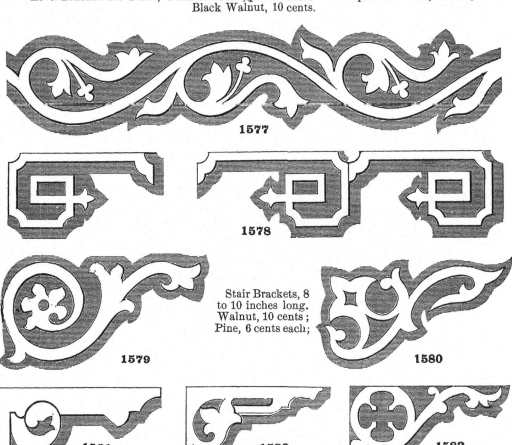

1577

1578

Stair Brackets, 8
to 10 inches long.
Walnut, 10 cents;
Pine, 6 cents each;

1579   1580

1581   1582   1583

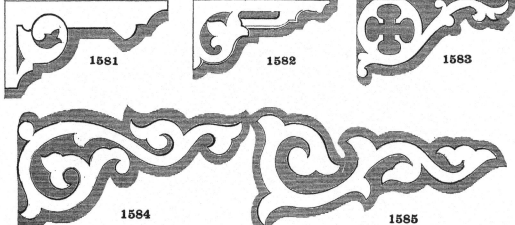

1584   1585

OUTSIDE RAILS.

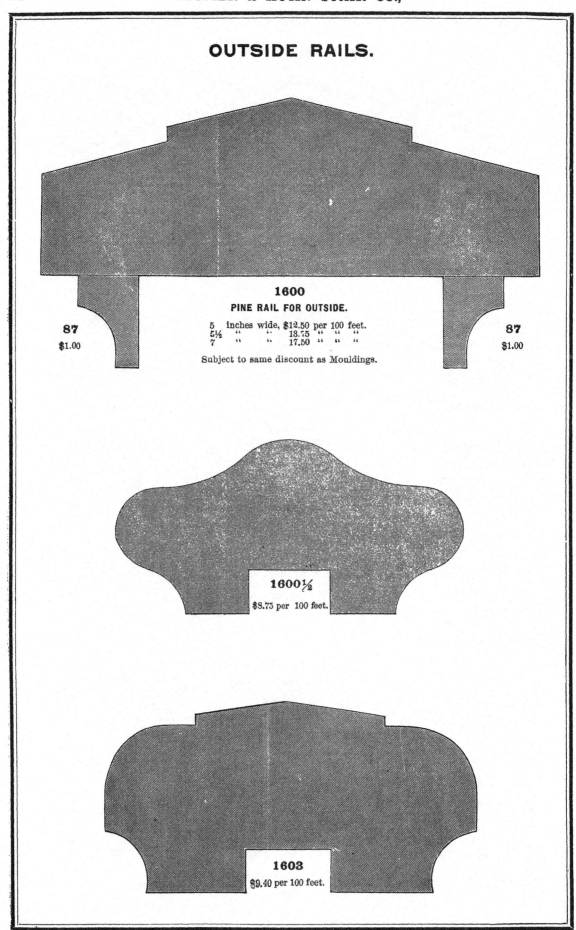

1600

PINE RAIL FOR OUTSIDE.

5   inches wide, $12.50 per 100 feet.
5½   "   "   13.75 "   "   "
7   "   "   17.50 "   "   "

Subject to same discount as Mouldings.

87
$1.00

87
$1.00

1600½

$8.75 per 100 feet.

1603

$9.40 per 100 feet.

RAILS AND BASE FOR OUTSIDE.

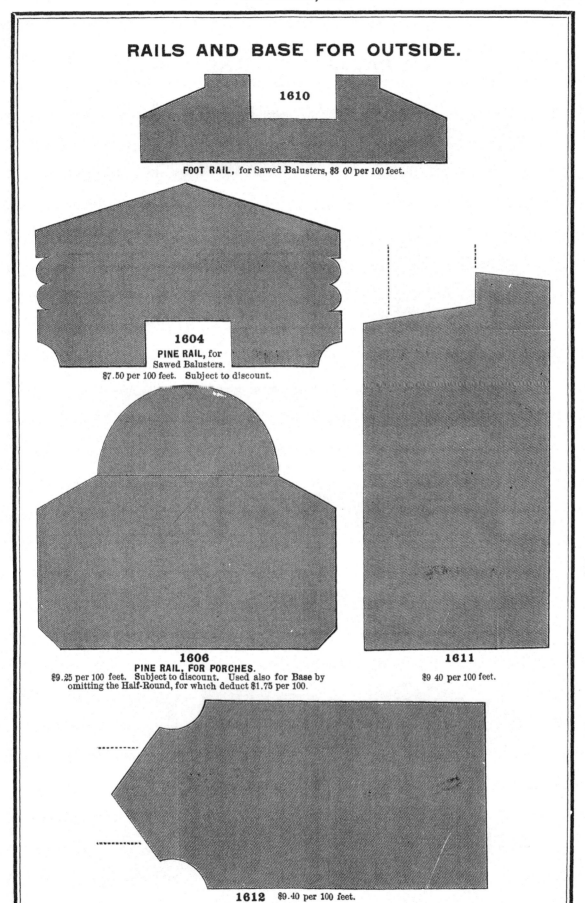

1610

FOOT RAIL, for Sawed Balusters, $3 00 per 100 feet.

1604
PINE RAIL, for
Sawed Balusters.
$7.50 per 100 feet.   Subject to discount.

1606
PINE RAIL, FOR PORCHES.
$9.25 per 100 feet.   Subject to discount.   Used also for Base by
omitting the Half-Round, for which deduct $1.75 per 100.

1611
$9 40 per 100 feet.

1612 $9.40 per 100 feet.

NEWELS FOR BALUSTRADE AND PORCH WORK.

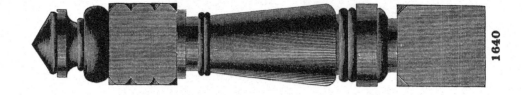

1640

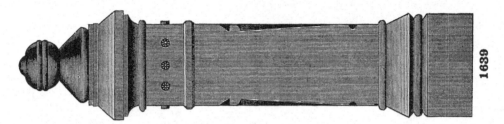

1639

FOR PRICES SEE PAGE 9.

1635

1634

1632

1631

1630

VERANDA POSTS.

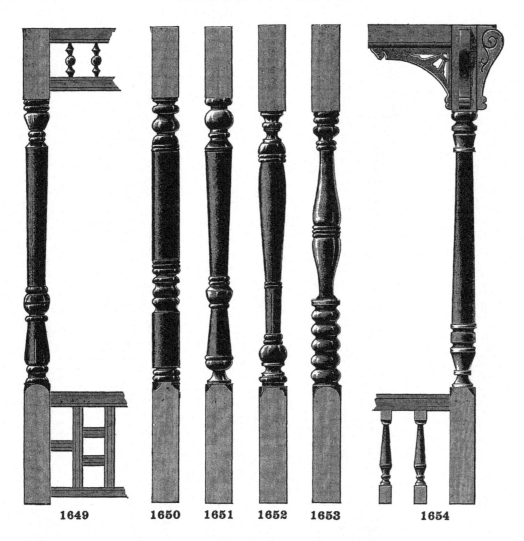

1649   1650   1651   1652   1653   1654

OUTSIDE BALUSTERS.

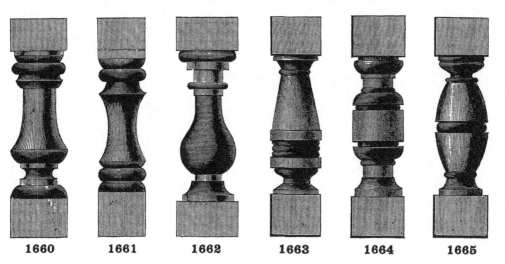

1660   1661   1662   1663   1664   1665

FOR PRICES SEE PAGE 9.

VERANDA POSTS.

We have in stock Turned Poplar Columns No. 1646 as follows :

4 x 4 in.— 8 ft.   32 in. square at bottom, 20 in. square at top.
4 x 4 in.— 9 ft.   34 in. square at bottom, 22 in. square at top.
4 x 4 in.—10 ft.   36 in. square at bottom, 24 in. square at top.

5 x 5 in.— 9 ft.   34 in. square at bottom, 22 in. square at top.
5 x 5 in.—10 ft.   36 in. square at bottom, 24 in. square at top.
6 x 6 in.—10 ft.   36 in. square at bottom, 24 in. square at top.

The above are made of first quality seasoned poplar.   Second quality Columns turned to order at reduced prices.

1645   **1646**   **1648**   **1648½**

PRICES SENT ON APPLICATION.

PORCH COLUMNS.

1655   1656   1657   1658

SPINDLES.

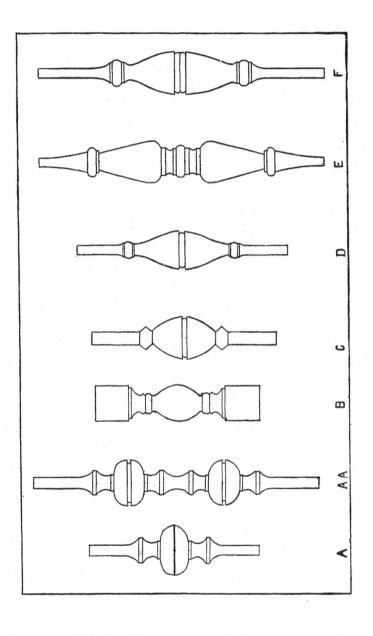

TURNED AND SAWED OUTSIDE BALUSTERS.

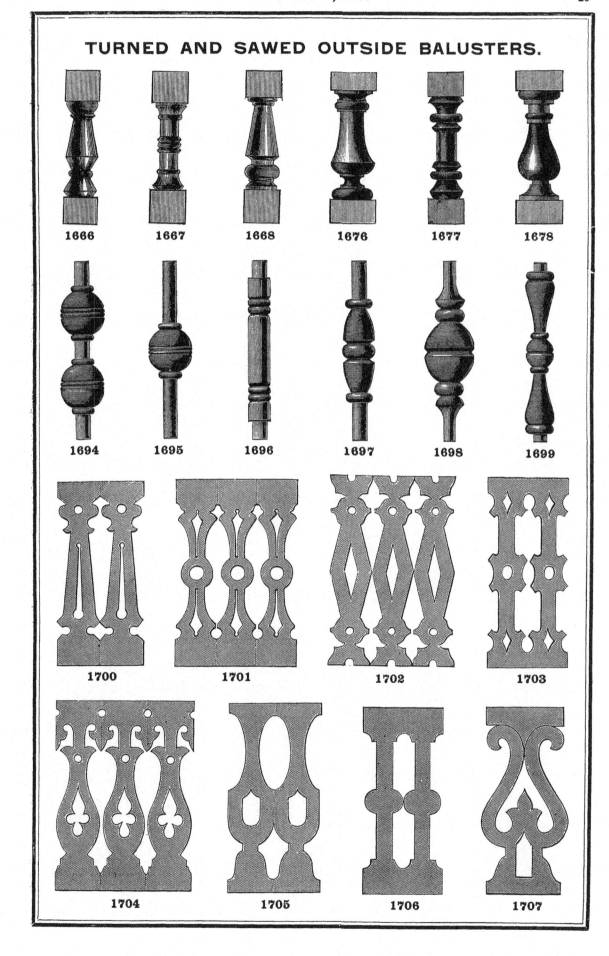

1666   1667   1668   1676   1677   1678

1694   1695   1696   1697   1698   1699

1700   1701   1702   1703

1704   1705   1706   1707

SAWED OUTSIDE BALUSTERS.

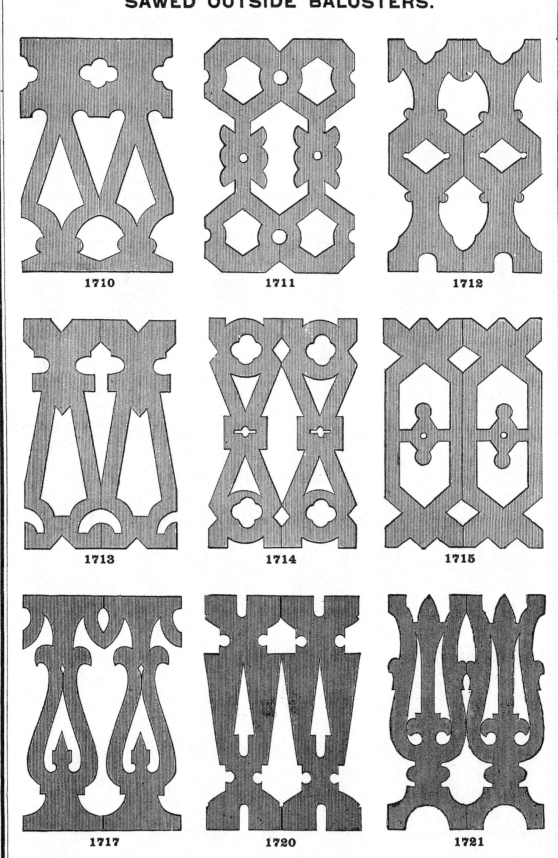

1710   1711   1712

1713   1714   1715

1717   1720   1721

VERANDAS.

1750

1751

1752

1753

VERANDAS.

1754

1755

1756

VERANDAS.

1757

1758
WRITE FOR PRICES.

VERANDAS.

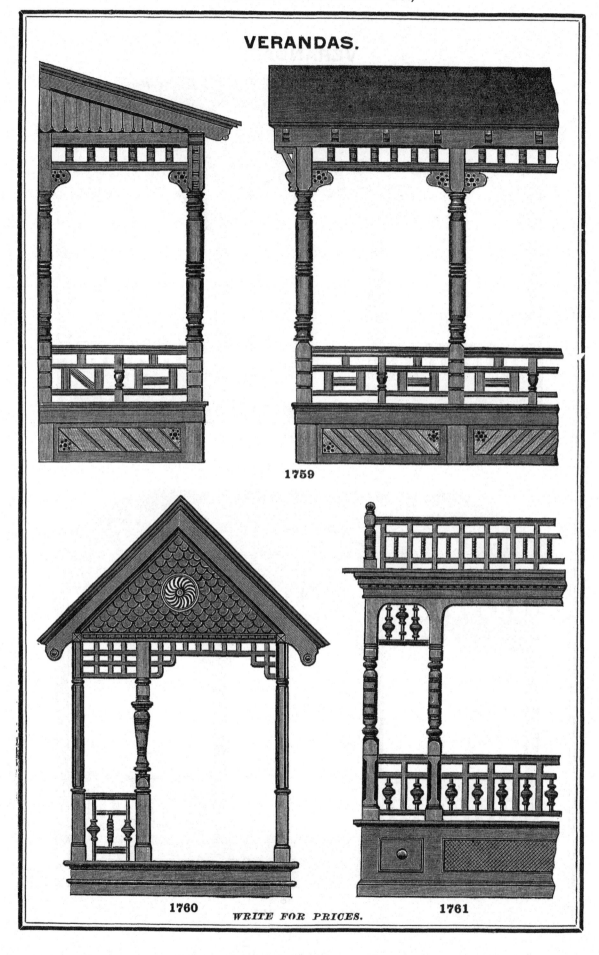

1759

1760   *WRITE FOR PRICES.*   1761

VERANDAS.

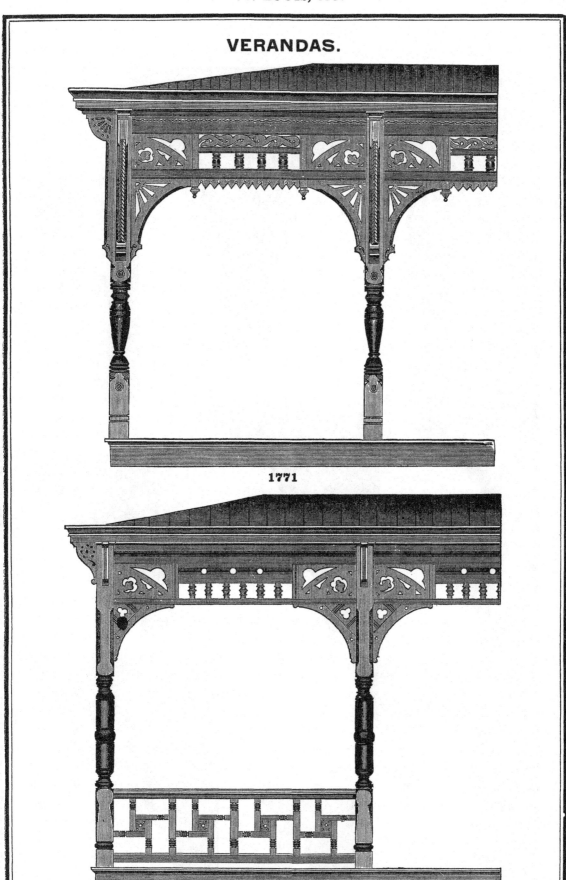

1771

1772
WRITE FOR PRICES.

BRACKETS.

BRACKETS.

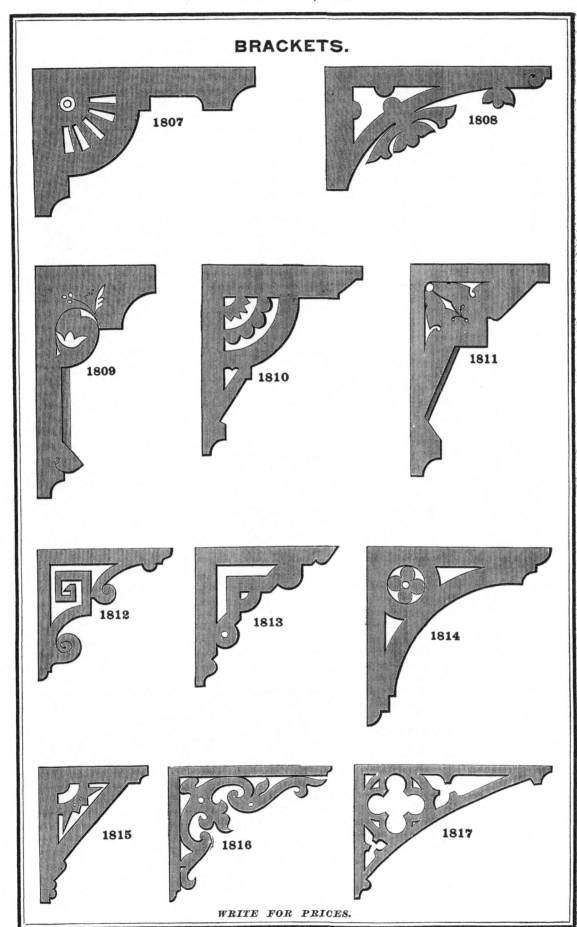

BRACKETS.

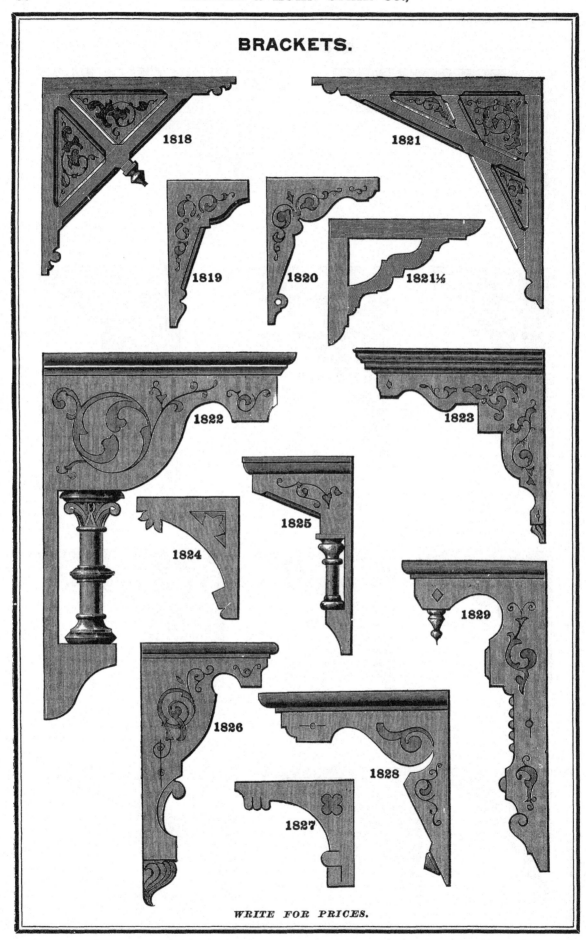

BRACKETS.

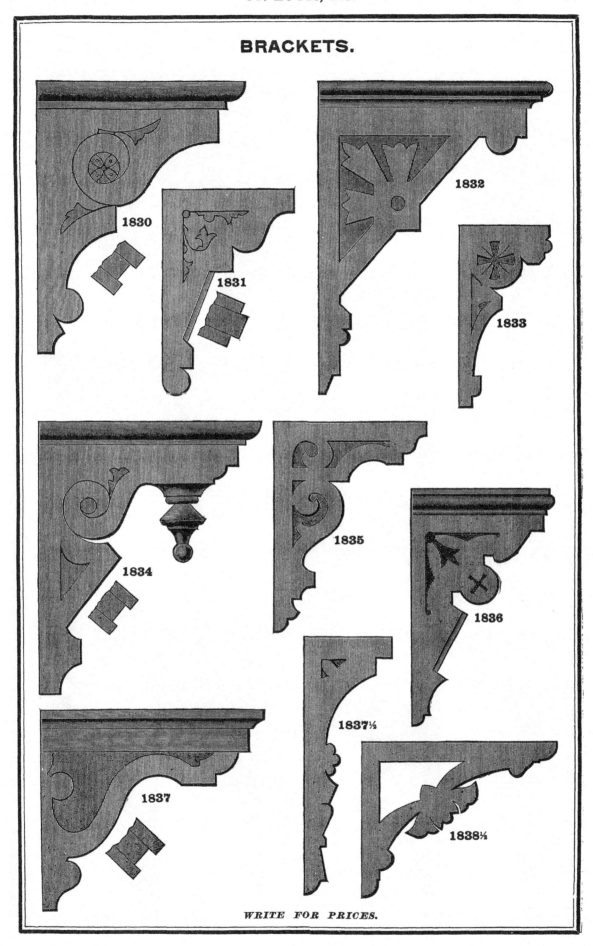

BRACKETS.

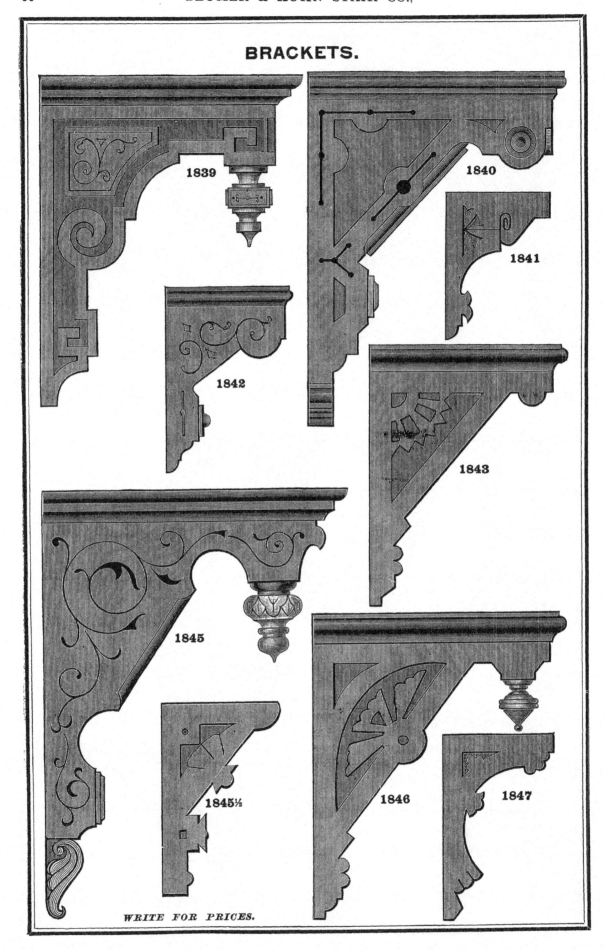

WRITE FOR PRICES.

WINDOW HOODS AND BRACKETS.

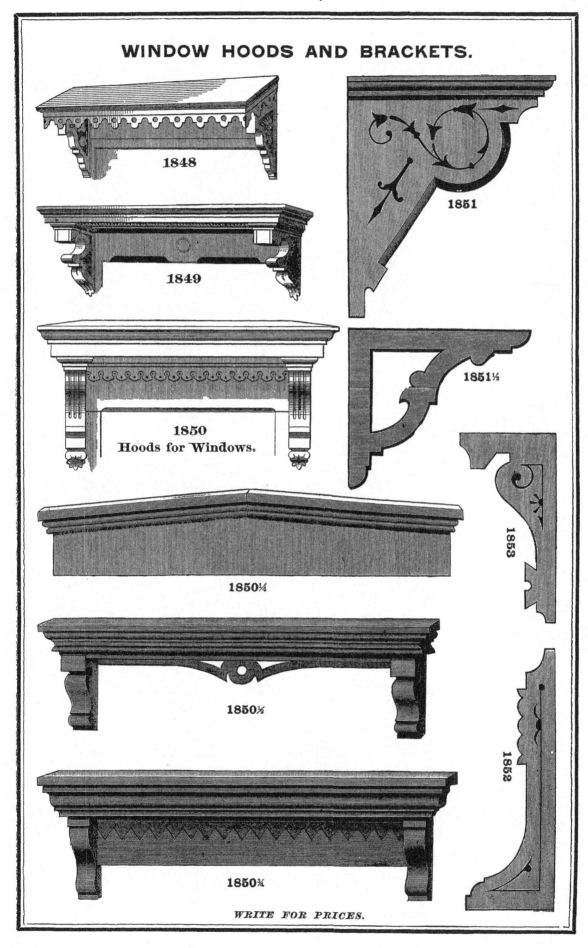

1848

1849

1850
Hoods for Windows.

1850¼

1850½

1850¾

1851

1851½

1853

1852

BRACKETS.

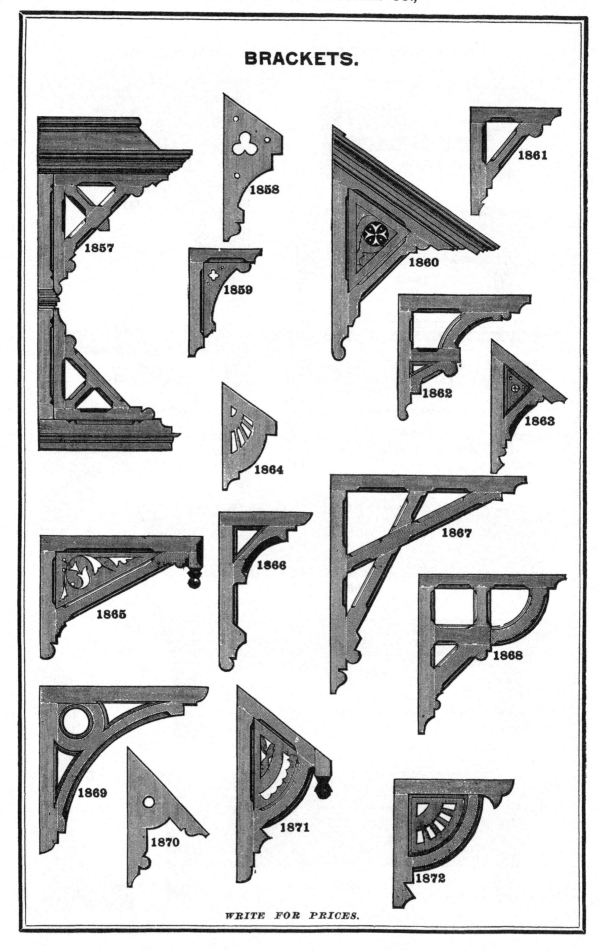

WRITE FOR PRICES.

BRACKETS.

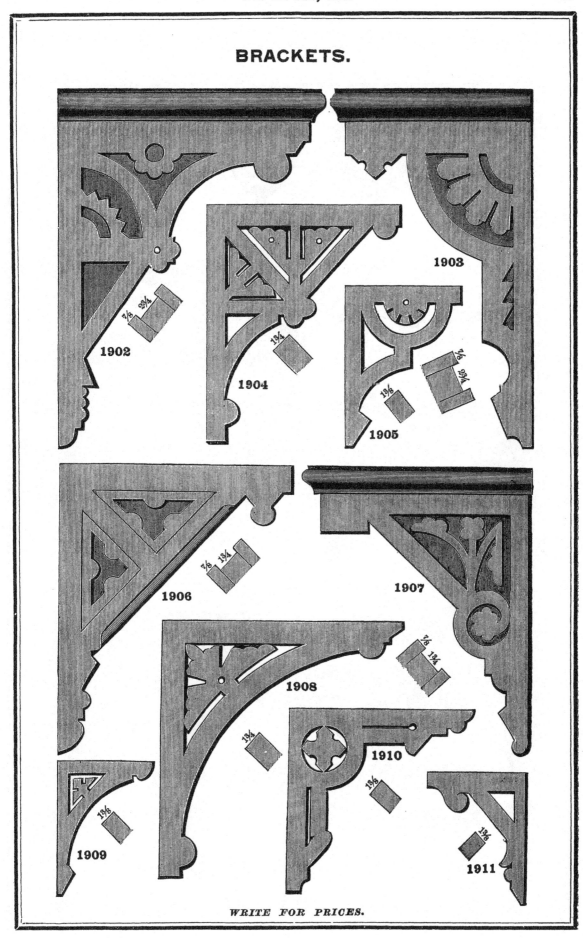

BRACKETS.

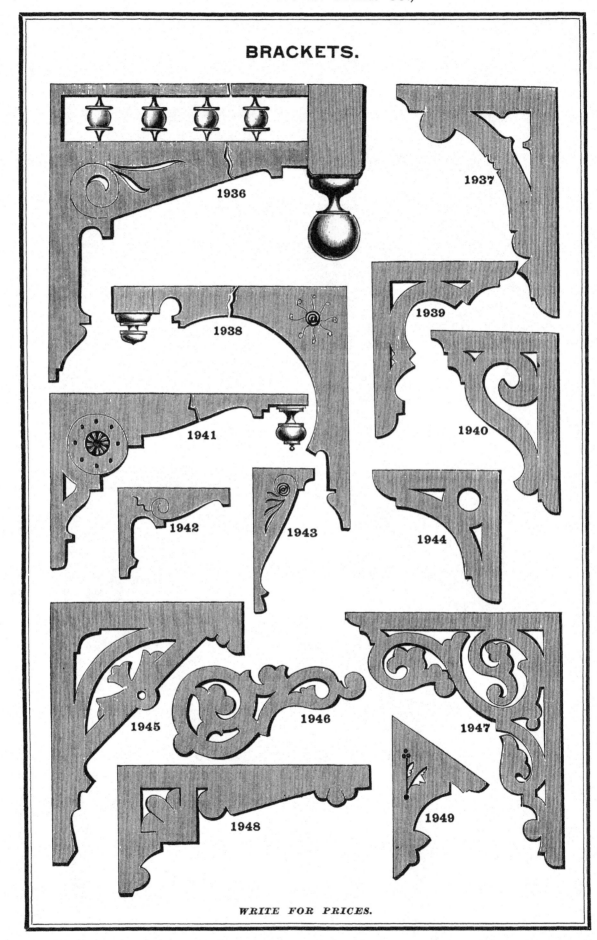

GABLE FINISH.

2014

2015

2016

2017

2018

2019

2020

2021

2022

2023

CORNICE DRAPERY, VERGE BOARDS, ETC.

GABLE FINISH AND WOOD ROSETTES.

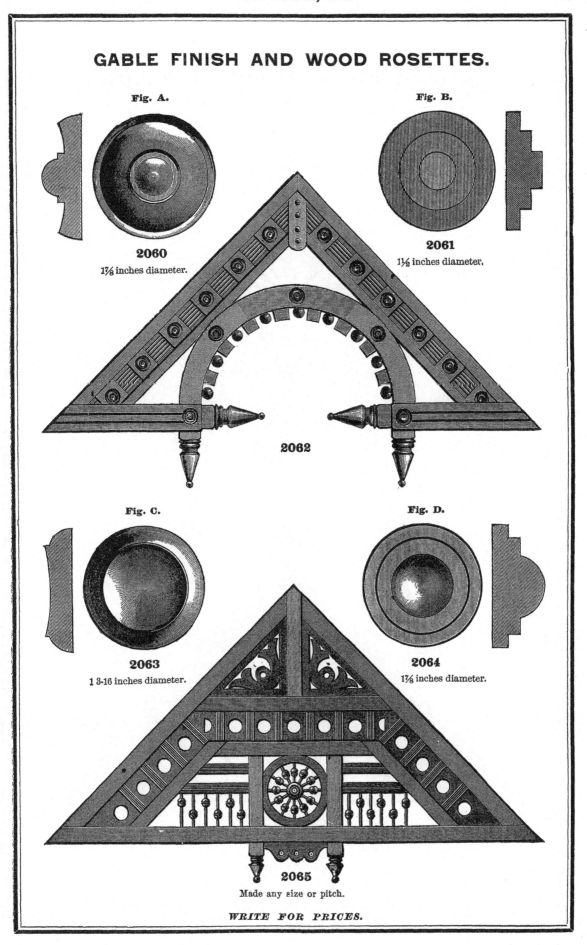

Fig. A.

2060

1⅞ inches diameter.

Fig. B.

2061

1½ inches diameter.

2062

Fig. C.

2063

1 3-16 inches diameter.

Fig. D.

2064

1⅞ inches diameter.

2065

Made any size or pitch.

WRITE FOR PRICES.

GABLE FINISH AND WOOD ROSETTES.

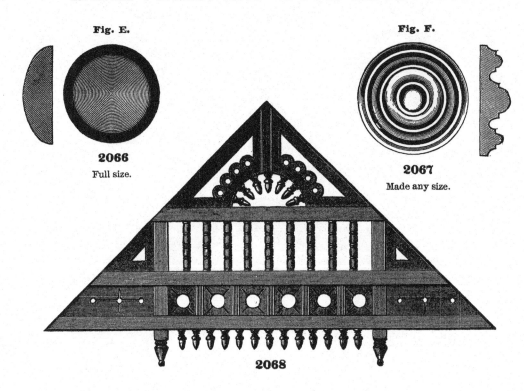

Fig. E.

2066

Full size.

Fig. F.

2067

Made any size.

2068

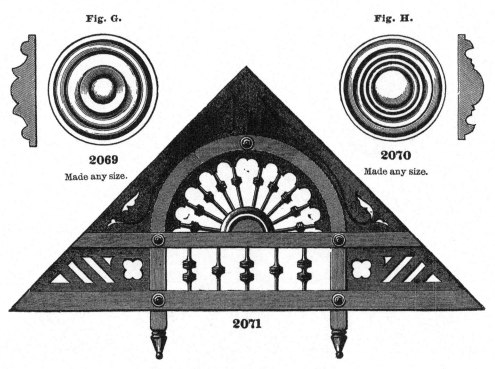

Fig. G.

2069

Made any size.

Fig. H.

2070

Made any size.

2071

Made any size or pitch.

GABLE FINISH AND WOOD ROSETTES.

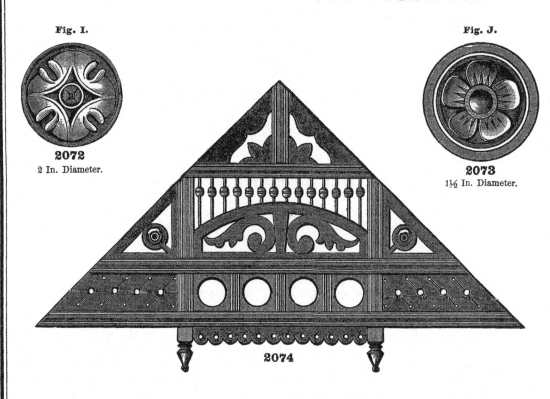

Fig. I.

2072
2 In. Diameter.

Fig. J.

2073
1½ In. Diameter.

2074

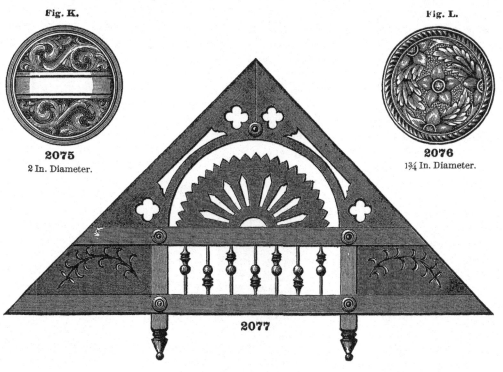

Fig. K.

2075
2 In. Diameter.

Fig. L.

2076
1¾ In. Diameter.

2077

Made any size or pitch.

CORNER AND BASE BEADS.

Corner Bead, No. **690**
1⅜ inch and 1¾ inch, 4 feet long, carried in stock.

Base Bead, No. **698**
1⅜ × 12½.

Base Bead, No. **699**
1⅜ × 14½.

CORNER, PLINTH, AND HEAD BLOCKS.

We manufacture *CORNER AND PLINTH BLOCKS* in a great variety of patterns, and give following a few cuts of styles with prices. The prices given are for *White and Yellow Pine* by the hundred. Red Oak or Birch are 50 per cent. higher, and Walnut 100 per cent. higher than marked prices. We also furnish *Carved* Corner or Plinth Blocks in endless varieties, at a small additional cost over those turned.

☞ *We sell Blocks in quantity desired. A liberal Discount to Dealers.*

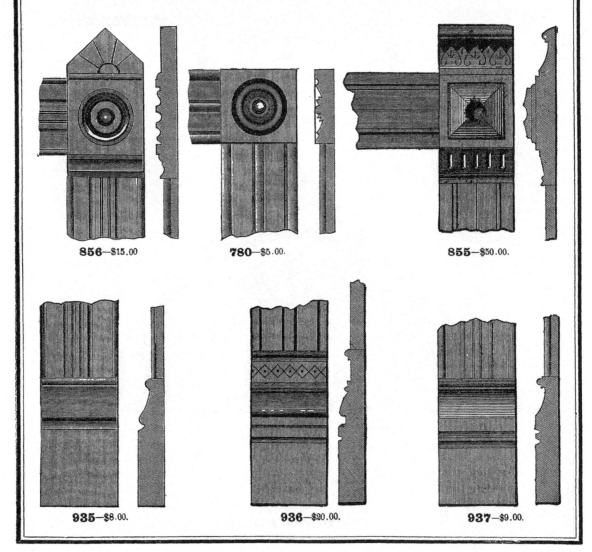

856—$15.00.　　　780—$5.00.　　　855—$50.00.

935—$8.00.　　　936—$20.00.　　　937—$9.00.

WOOD CORNER BLOCKS.

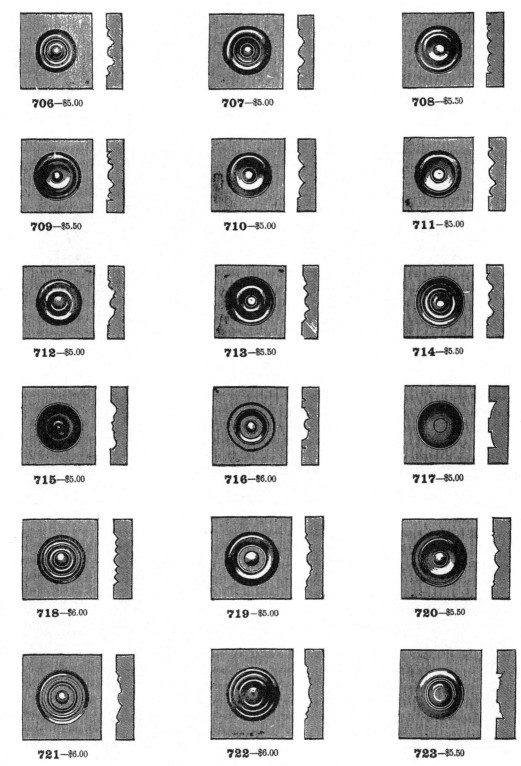

706—$5.00   707—$5.00   708—$5.50

709—$5.50   710—$5.00   711—$5.00

712—$5.00   713—$5.50   714—$5.50

715—$5.00   716—$6.00   717—$5.00

718—$6.00   719—$5.00   720—$5.50

721—$6.00   722—$6.00   723—$5.50

Above prices are for Blocks from 4×4 to $6 \times 6 \times 1\frac{1}{8}$ inches thick.
Prices are for White Pine by the hundred.

WOOD CORNER BLOCKS.

724

4½ to 6 in. $10.00

725

4½ to 6 in. $10.00

726

4½ to 6 in. $7.00

727

4½ to 6 in. $7.00

728

4½ to 6 in. $20.00

729

4½ to 6 in. $20.00

730

4½ to 6 in. $7.00

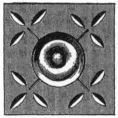

731

4½ to 6 in. $6.50

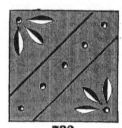

732

4½ to 6 in. $5.50

733

4½ to 6 in. $20.00

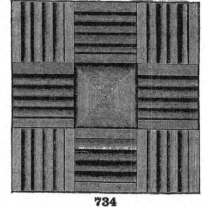

734

4½ to 6 in. $20.00

Prices are for White Pine by the hundred for Blocks 1⅛ inches thick.

WOOD CORNER BLOCKS.

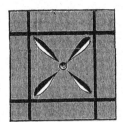

735

4½ to 6 in. × 1⅛, $5.50

736

4½ to 6 in. × 1⅛, $6.50

736½

4½ to 6 in. × 1⅛, $6.00

737

4½ to 6 in. × 1⅛, $6.50

739

4½ to 6 in. × 1⅛, $6.50

738

4½ to 6 in. × 1⅛, $5.50

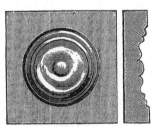

740

4½ to 6 in. × 1⅛, $5.50

741

4½ to 6 in. × 1⅛, $25.00

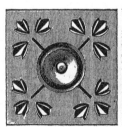

742

4½ to 6 in. × 1⅛, $8.50

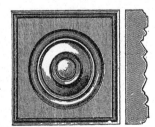

743

4½ to 6 in. × 1⅛, $7.00

744

4½ to 6 in. × 1⅛, Hand Carved, $110.00

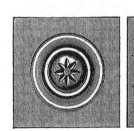

745

4½ to 6 in. × 1⅛, $6.50

WOOD CORNER BLOCKS.

747
4½ to 6 × 1⅛, $25.00

748
4½ to 6 × 1⅛, $18.00

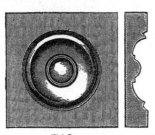

749
4½ to 6 × 1⅛, $5.00

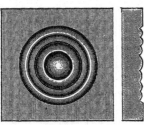

750
4½ to 6 × 1⅛, $5.50

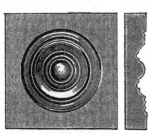

751
4½ to 6 × 1⅛, $6.00

752

SIZE.	Thickness.	Price per 100.
4½ to 5¾ In. Square.	1⅛	$15.00
6 to 6¾ " "	"	18.00
5 to 5¾ " "	1⅜	18.00
6 to 6¾ " "	"	20.00

753
Prices same as No. 752 above.

WOOD CORNER BLOCKS AND ORNAMENTS.

756

SIZE.	Thickness.	Price per 100.
4½ to 5¾ In. Square.	1⅛	$15.00
6 to 6¾ " "	"	18.00
5 to 5¾ " "	1⅜	18.00
6 to 6¾ " "	"	20 00

754

1⅝ × 8, $12.50 per 100

757

Sizes and prices same as No. 756.

755

3⅛ × 2½, $8.00 per 100

2¾ × 4½, $13.00 per 100

WOOD CORNER BLOCKS AND ORNAMENTS.

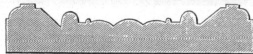

758

Price same as No. 756.

759

SIZE.		Thickness.	Price per 100.
5 to 6 In. Square		1⅛	$25.00
6 to 6¾ " "		1⅜	30.00
7 to 8½ " "		"	35.00
6 to 6¾ " "		1¾	35.00
7 to 8¼ " "		"	38.00

760

4 In. Diameter. $18.00 per 100

761

3¾ In. Square. $18.00 per 100
4¾ In. Square.   25.00 per 100

762

2¾ × 6 In. $25.00 per 100
3¾ × 8 In.   30.00 per 100

WOOD ORNAMENTS.

763

764

765

766

767

768

769

770

771

PRICES OF ABOVE ORNAMENTS.

No.	Size.		Per 100.	No.	Size.		Per 100.
763	1	inches diameter.	$1.50	765	2⅜ inches square.		$ 5.50
763	1¼	" "	2.00	766	1⅞	" "	4.25
763	1½	" "	2.50	767	1¾	" diameter.	3.00
763	1¾	" "	3.00	768	1⅞	" square.	4.25
763	2	" "	3.75	768	2⅜	" "	6.00
763	2¼	" "	4.50	768	3¼	" "	15.00
763	2½	" "	5.50	769	1¾	" "	3.75
763	2¾	" "	6.50	770	1¾	" diameter.	3.00
763	3¼	" "	7.50	770	2½	" "	6.50
764	1	" "	2.00	771	1⅛	" "	2.00
764	1¼	" "	3.00	771	1⅜	" "	2.50
764	1½	" "	3.75	771	1⅝	" "	3.00
764	1¾	" "	4.25	771	2¼	" "	4.50
764	2	" "	4.50				

WOOD CORNER BLOCKS.

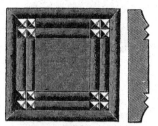

776

4½ to 6 in. sq. × 1⅜ $9.00 per 100

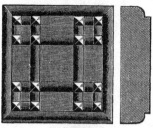

777

4½ to 6 in. sq. × 1⅜ $15.00 per 100

778

4½ to 6 in. sq. × 1⅛ $10.00 per 100

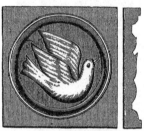

779

4½ to 6 in. sq. × 1⅛ $20.00 per 100

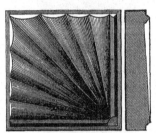

787

5 to 6 in. sq. × 1⅛ $15.00 per 100

788

5 to 6 in. sq. × 1⅛ $25.00 per 100

791

5 to 6 in. sq. × 1⅛ $10.00 per 100

792

5 to 6 in. sq. × 1⅛ $7.00 per 100

793

5 to 6 in. sq. × 1⅛ $7.00 per 100

794

5 to 6 in. sq. × 1⅛ $6.50 per 100

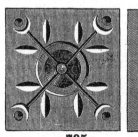

795

5 to 6 in. sq. × 1⅛ $7.50 per 100

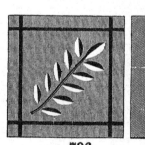

796

5 to 6 in. sq. × 1⅛ $6.00 per 100

WOOD CORNER BLOCKS.

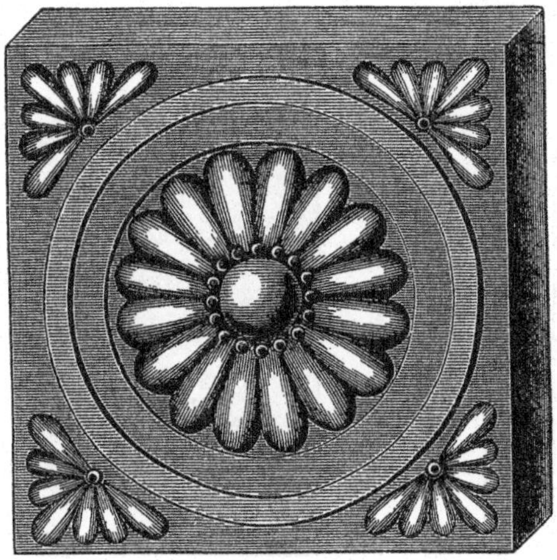

798–A
5⅜ inches square, $42.00 per 100

798–B
5⅜ and 5¾ inches square, $42.00 per 100

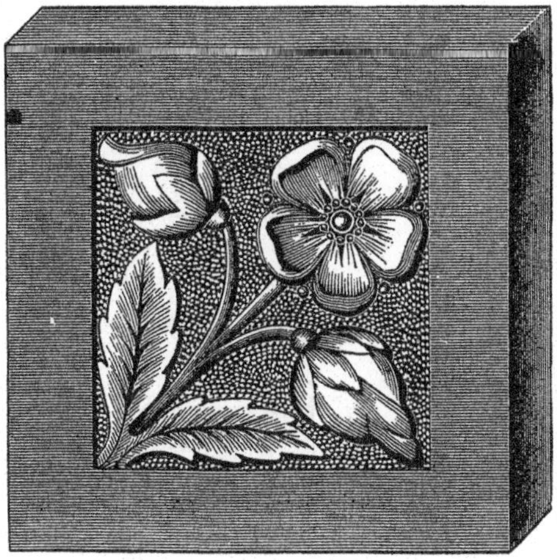

798–C
5⅜ and 5¾ inches square, $42.00 per 100

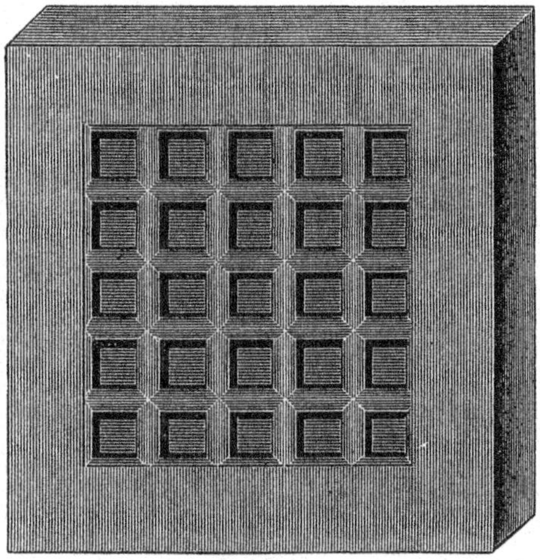

798–D
5⅜ and 5¾ inches square, $42.00 per 100

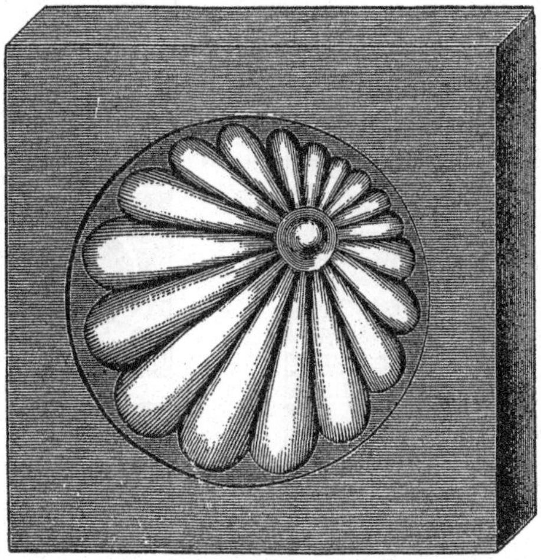

798–E
5⅜ and 5¾ inches square, $42.00 per 100

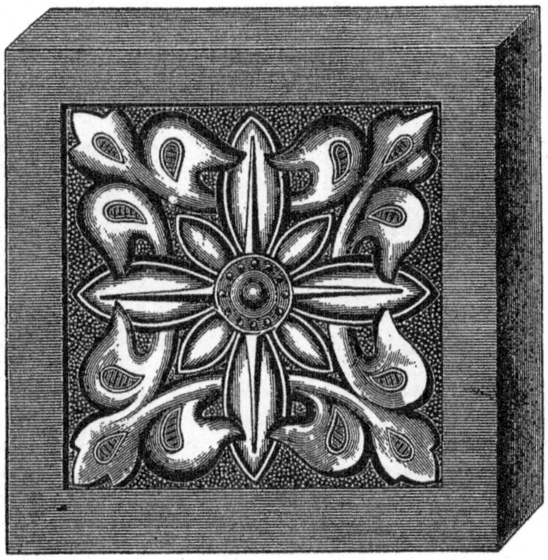

798–F
5⅜ and 5¾ inches square, $42.00 per 100

WOOD HEAD BLOCKS.

802

5½×10, $10.00 per 100

803

5½×10, $18.00 per 100

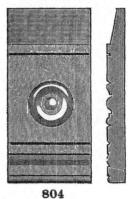

804

5½×10, $10.00 per 100

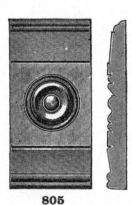

805

5½×10, $11.00 per 100

806

5½×11, $15.00 per 100

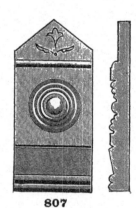

807

5½×11, $16.00 per 100

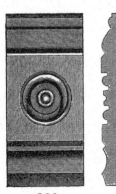

809

5½×10, $10.00 per 100

810

5½×10, $10.00 per 100

811

5½×12, $14.00 per 100

812

5½×12, $16.00 per 100

Above Blocks are 1⅛ inches thick.

WOOD HEAD BLOCKS.

814
5½×11, $13.00 per 100

815
5½×11, $11.00 per 100

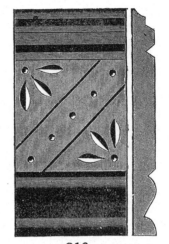

816
5½×11, $11.00 per 100

817
5½×10, $12.00 per 100

818
5½×10, $11.00 per 100

819
5½×12, $12.00 per 100

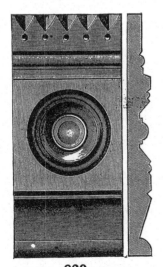

820
5½×12, $15.00 per 100

821
5½×9½, $12.00 per 100

822
5½×10, $30.00 per 100

Above Blocks are 1⅛ inches thick.

WOOD HEAD BLOCKS.

823
5½ × 10, $17.00 per 100

824
5½ × 10, $12.00 per 100

825
5½ × 11, hand carved, $120.00 per 100

825—A
3 inches Square, $16.00 per 100

825—B
3½ inches Square, $17.00 per 100

825—C
3 inches Square, $17.00 per 100

825—A, B, and C are Pressed Wood Ornaments, which can be used for center pieces of Corner or Head Blocks, at greatly reduced price over hand carving, and equally as effective.

826
5½ × 10, $12.00 per 100

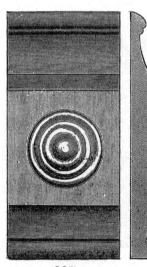

827
5½ × 10½, $11.00 per 100

828
5½ × 10, $11.00 per 100

WOOD HEAD BLOCKS.

829

5½ × 10½ × 1⅛, $30.00 per 100

830

5½ × 11 × 1⅛, $20.00 per 100

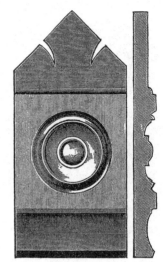

831

5½ × 10½ × 1⅛, $14.00 per 100

832

5 to 5¾ × 9 × 1⅜ thick, $40.00
6 to 6¾ × 10 × 1⅜ " 45.00

833

5 to 5¾ × 13 × 1⅜ thick, $50.00
6 to 6¾ × 13 × 1⅜ " 60.00
7 to 8 × 13 × 1⅜ " 75.00

832—A

2½ in. Square, $9.00 per 100

Can be used as Center for
Head Blocks.

WOOD HEAD BLOCKS.

834

5½ × 12½, $60.00 per 100

835

5½ × 11½, $13 00 per 100

836

5½ × 12, $24 00 per 100

836—A　　　　　　**836—B**　　　　　　**836—C**

836—A, B, and C are Wood Ornaments, which can be used with good effect for centers of Corners and Head Blocks.

837

5½ × 12, $50.00 per 100

839

5½ × 12½, $25.00 per 100

844

5½ × 12, $55.00 per 100

WOOD BASE OR PLINTH BLOCKS.

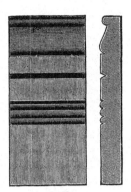

900

5½ × 10 × 1⅜, $11.00 per 100

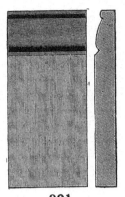

901

5½ × 9 × 1⅜, $8.00 per 100

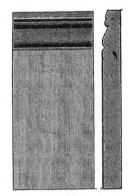

902

5½ × 9 × 1⅜, $9.00 per 100

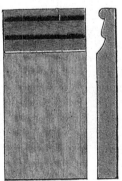

903

5½ × 8 × 1⅜, $8.00 per 100

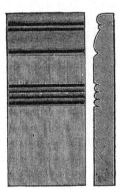

904

5½ × 10 × 1⅜, $11.00 per 100

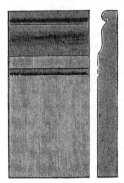

905

5½ × 10 × 1⅜, $9 00 per 100

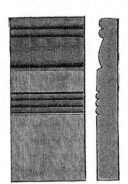

906

5½ × 10 × 1⅜, $11.00 per 100

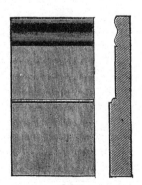

907

5½ × 10 × 1⅜, $10.00 per 100

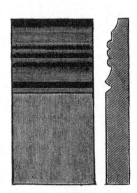

908

5½ × 10 × 1⅜, $10.00 per 100

WOOD BASE OR PLINTH BLOCKS.

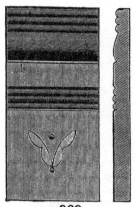

909
5½ × 12 × 1⅜, $12.00 per 100

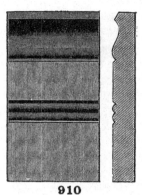

910
5½ × 10 × 1⅜, $10.00 per 100

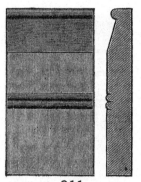

911
5½ × 10 × 1⅜, $10.00 per 100

912
5½ × 10 × 1⅜, $10.00 per 100

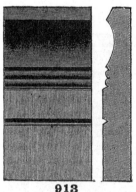

913
5½ × 10 × 1⅜, $11.00 per 100

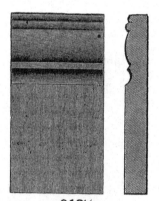

913½
5½ × 10 × 1⅜, $9.50 per 100

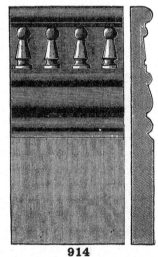

914
5½×12×1⅜, $20.00 per 100

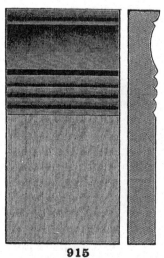

915
5½×11×1⅜, $11.00 per 100

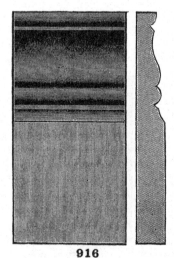

916
5½×11×1⅜, $11.00 per 100

WOOD BASE OR PLINTH BLOCKS.

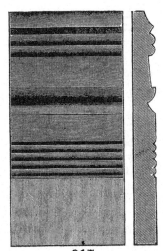

917
5½×11×1⅜, $13.00 per 100

918
5½×12×1⅜, $13.00 per 100

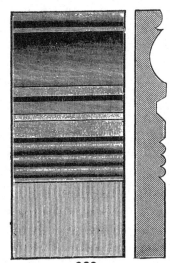

929
5½×12×1⅜, $13.00 per 100

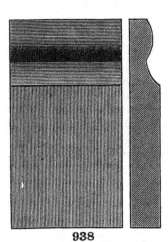

938
5½×10×1⅜, $8.00 per 100

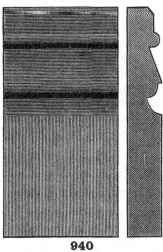

940
5½×11×1⅜, $9.50 per 100

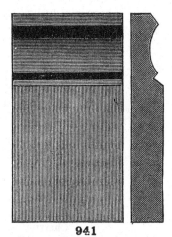

941
5½×10×1⅜, $8.00 per 100

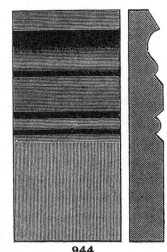

944
5½×11×1⅜, $9.00 per 100

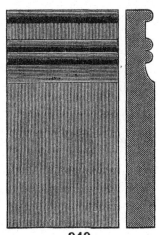

949
5½×10×1⅜, $8.00 per 100

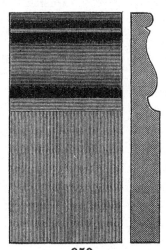

950
5½×12×1⅜, $9.50 per 100

HARDWOOD MANTELS.

ON PAGES 89 TO 110, INCLUSIVE, ARE SHOWN A FEW DESIGNS THAT HAVE BEEN SELECTED AS MEETING THE POPULAR DEMAND.

SIZE. Stock size of all Mantels is 5 feet, but Mantels can be widened to 5 feet 6 inches by extending the wall plates. We will always widen Mantels in this way unless otherwise specified. If Mantel is wider than 5 feet 6 inches, or narrower than 5 feet, an extra price will be charged.

WOOD. Mantels marked made only in Red Oak or Birch, are manufactured in large quantities in these two woods, and carried in stock, consequently we are enabled to list them at a very low price. They will be made to order in other woods, if desired, at special prices. All other designs are made in any of the native hardwoods (see below).

TILES. Enameled and Embossed Tiles come in nearly every shade and tint. Where colors of tiling are not specified, we always select those which harmonize best with the wood of the Mantel.

TRIMMINGS. We can furnish Brass and Wrought Iron goods, Andirons, Fenders, Fire Sets, Frames, Grates, and Portable Baskets, Iron Linings, etc., and can ship any of these goods with Mantels.

PRICES. We have made our prices in a way that will enable any one to arrange the Mantel they may select, with any of the trimmings shown in catalogue. Everything that is necessary to set the Mantel, just as shown in cut, is included, except 75 common brick and a little mortar. We name each article that we include.

In ordering, state width of chimney-breast, and kind of wood and finish wanted.

NATIVE WOODS.

Red Oak, natural or antique.
Birch, natural or stained mahogany.
Cherry, natural or antique.
Quarter-Sawed White Oak, natural or antique.
Quarter-Sawed Sycamore.
Gum Wood.
Ash, natural or antique.
Walnut.
California Red Wood.
White Maple.
Butternut.
Sixteenth Century Finish, Cremona Finish, and Old English Oak.

EXTRA WOODS.

Mahogany, natural or antique.
Prima Vera.
Bird's-Eye Maple.
Curly Birch.
White and Gold.

MANTELS.

2100

From 18 to 30 inches long.

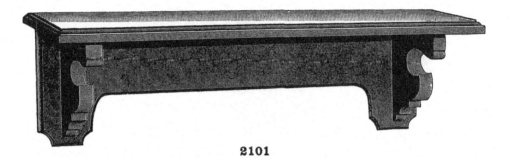

2101

2102

WRITE FOR PRICES.

MANTELS.

2103

From 30 to 48 inches long.

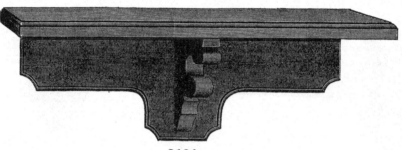

2104

2105

WRITE FOR PRICES.

MANTELS.

2106

2107

MANTELS.

2108

2109

WRITE FOR PRICES.

MANTEL.

2110

MANTEL.

2111

MANTEL.

2112

MANTEL.

2113

MANTEL.

2114

MANTEL.

2115

MANTEL.

2116

MANTEL.

2117

MANTEL.

2118

MANTEL.

2119

Length of Shelf.. 5 feet.
Width of Opening .... 2 " 11½ inches.
Width of Opening may be varied up to......................... 3 " 6 "
Height of Opening.. 2 " 11¾ "
Profile ....   4 "
Height of Mantel from floor to highest point .... 6 " 5 "
Size of Mirror .... 40 x 18 "
    If length of Shelf is increased, the size and cost of Mirror will be increased proportionately.

WRITE FOR PRICES.

MANTEL.

2120

Length of Shelf.. 5 feet.
Width of Opening .... 2 " 11¼ inches.
Width of Opening may be varied up to.................................. 3 " 6 "
Height of Opening... 2 " 11¼ "
Profile... 7 "
Height of Mantel from floor to highest point .... 6 "
Size of Mirror .... 40 x 12 "

If length of Shelf is increased, the size and cost of Mirror will be increased proportionately.

WRITE FOR PRICES.

MANTEL.

2121

Length of Shelf .... 5 feet.
Width of Opening .... 2 " 11½ inches.
Width of Opening may be varied up to............................... 3 " 6 "
Height of Opening... 2 " 11¾ "
Profile.. 8 "
Height of Mantel from floor to highest point................................. 6 " 8 "
Size of Mirror.. 28 x 20 "

If length of Shelf is increased, the size and cost of Mirror will be increased proportionately.

WRITE FOR PRICES.

MANTEL.

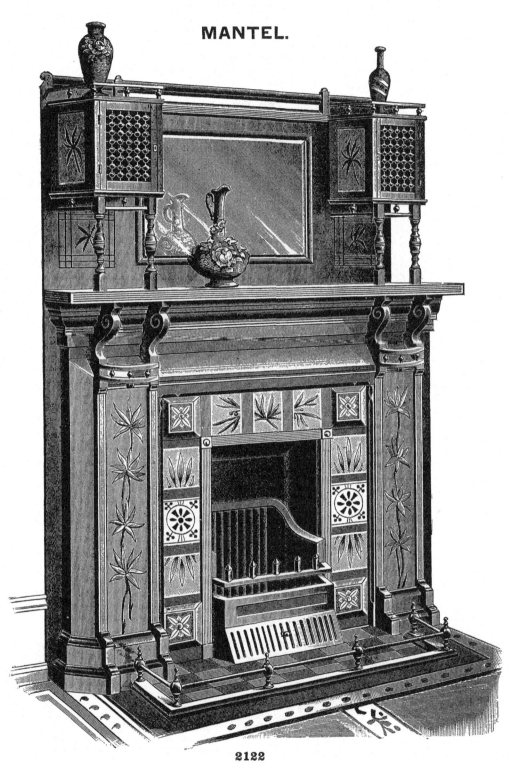

2122

Length of Shelf.. 5 feet.
Width of Opening .... 2 " 11½ inches.
    Width of Opening can not be increased without increasing length of Shelf.
Height of Opening.. 2 " 11¾ "
Profile............. .... 7 "
Height of Mantel from floor to highest point...................... 6 ' 5 '"
Size of Mirror.. 28 x 20 "

WRITE FOR PRICES.

MANTEL.

2123

Length of Shelf... 5 feet.
Width of Opening .... 2 " 11½ inches.
Height of Opening.. 2 " 11¼ "
By moving back Side Linings, width of Opening may be varied up to........... 3 " 6 "

MANTEL.

2124

Length of Shelf.. 5 feet.
Width of Opening .... 2 " 11½ inches.
Height of Opening.. 2 " 11¾ "

WRITE FOR PRICES.

MANTEL.

2125

Length of Shelf... 5 feet.
Width of Opening .... 2 " 11½ inches.
Height of Opening.. 2 " 11¾ "

MANTEL.

2126

Length of Shelf.. 5 feet.
Width of Opening... 2 " 11½ inches.
Height of Opening... 2 " 11¼ "

WRITE FOR PRICES.

MANTEL.

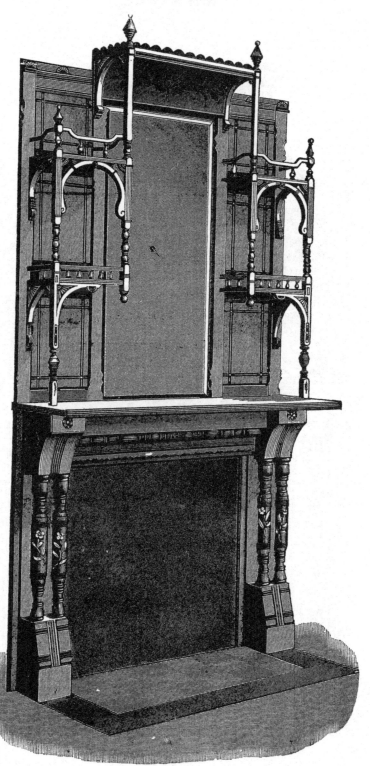

2127

Length of Shelf .... 5 feet.
Width of Opening... 2 " 11½ inches.
Height of Opening.. 2 " 11¾ "
By moving back Side Linings, width of Opening may be varied up to..... ...... 3 " 6 "

WRITE FOR PRICES.

OFFICE AND BANK COUNTERS.

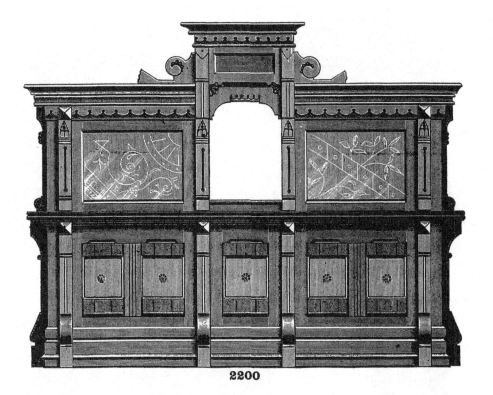

2200

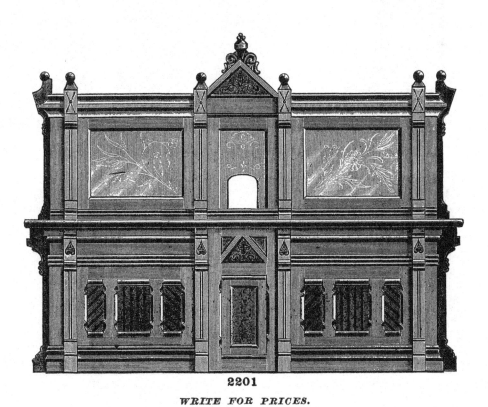

2201

WRITE FOR PRICES.

PULPITS.

2225

2226

2227

2228

2232

2233

PEW ENDS.

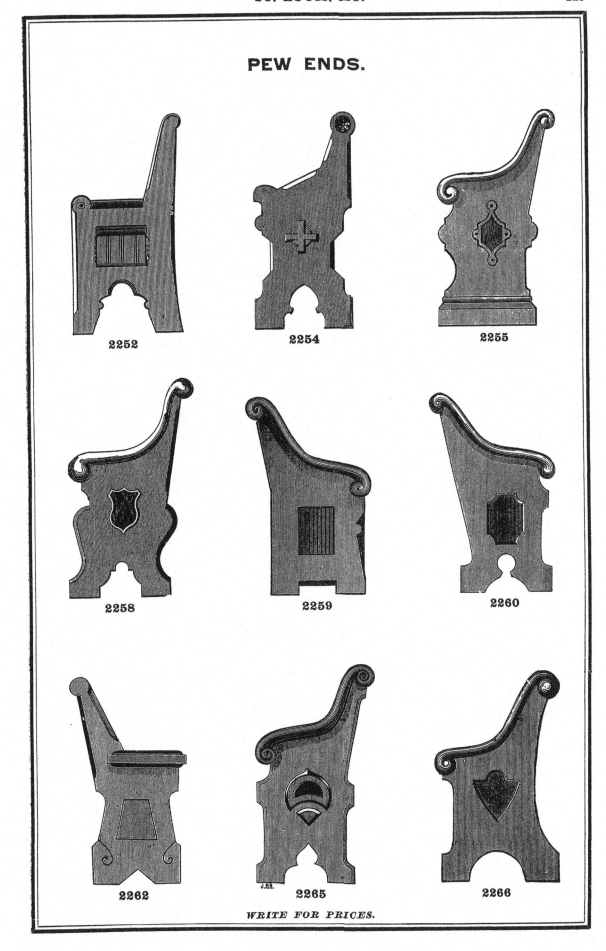

2252   2254   2255

2258   2259   2260

2262   2265   2266

J.ER.

WRITE FOR PRICES.

Interior Hardwood Finish.

WE would especially call your attention to our revised list of the latest styles of Mouldings, as shown on pages Nos. 115 to 136 inclusive. We make a specialty of furnishing these, in any kind of hardwood, either in large or small quantities. Also, if you should fancy a design from some other catalogue, by sending sketch or detail of same, it will be furnished you as cheerfully as if selected from our catalogue, and at as reasonable prices.

Any information in assisting you in ordering your goods in conformity to our designs, and to apply to your particular work, will be cheerfully sent you on application.

Yours respectfully,

BLUMER & KUHN STAIR CO.

CASINGS.

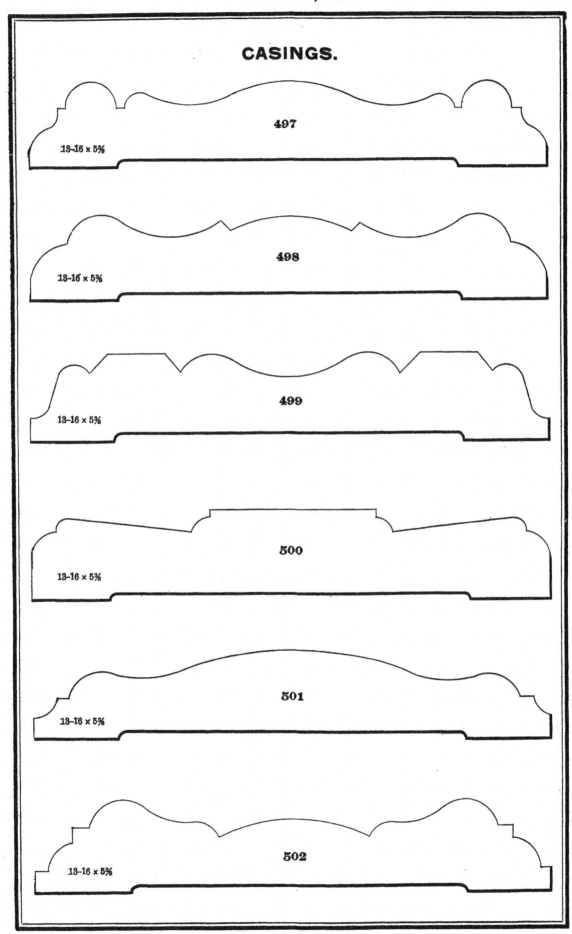

CASINGS.

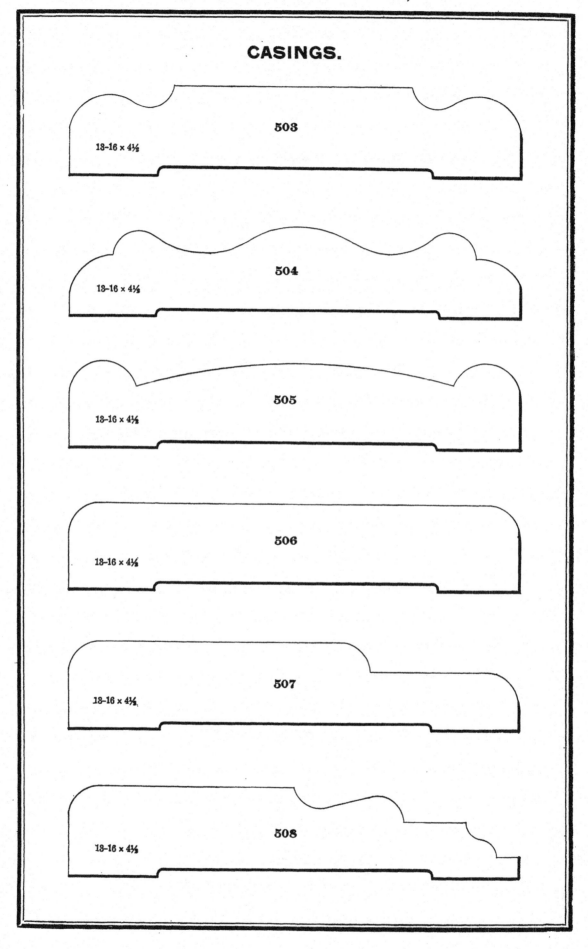

503

13–16 × 4½

504

13–16 × 4½

505

13–16 × 4½

506

13–16 × 4½

507

13–16 × 4½

508

13–16 × 4½

EASTLAKE AND QUEEN ANNE CASINGS.

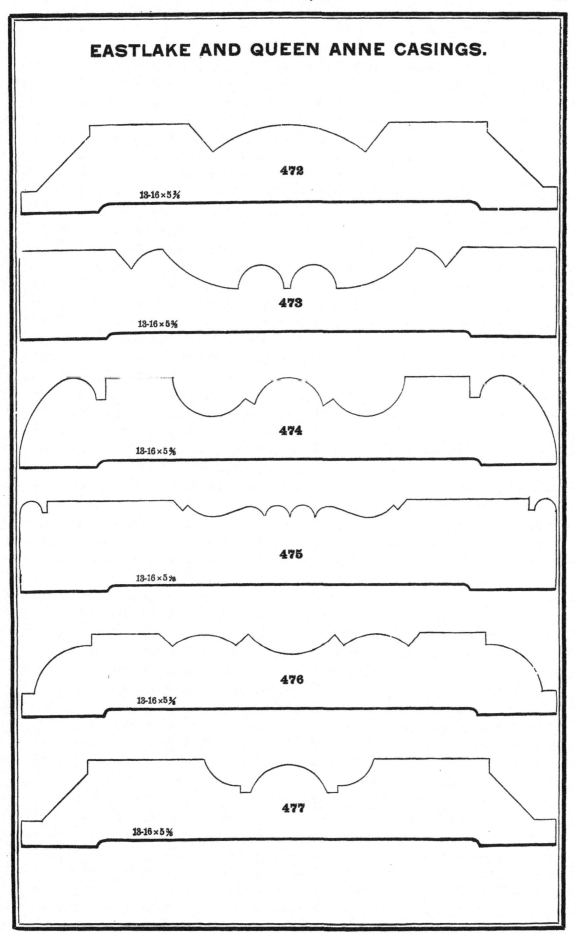

472

13-16×5¾

473

13-16×5⅝

474

13-16×5⅝

475

13-16×5⅞

476

13-16×5¾

477

13-16×5⅝

CASINGS.

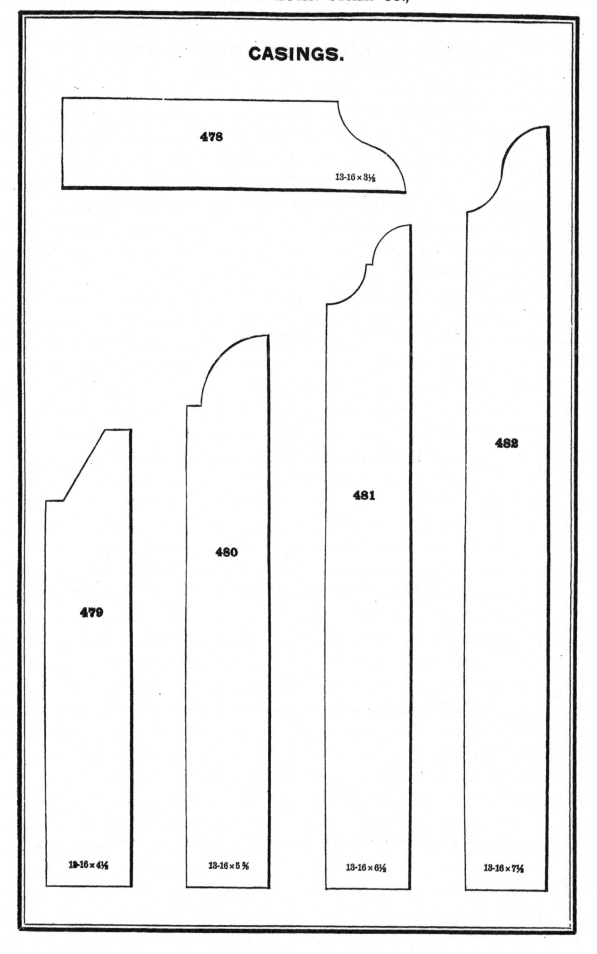

478   13-16 × 3½

479   13-16 × 4½

480   13-16 × 5⅝

481   13-16 × 6½

482   13-16 × 7½

CASINGS.

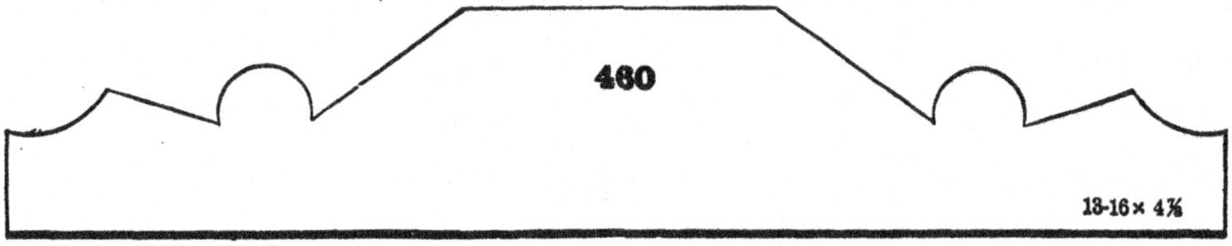
460
13-16 × 4⅝

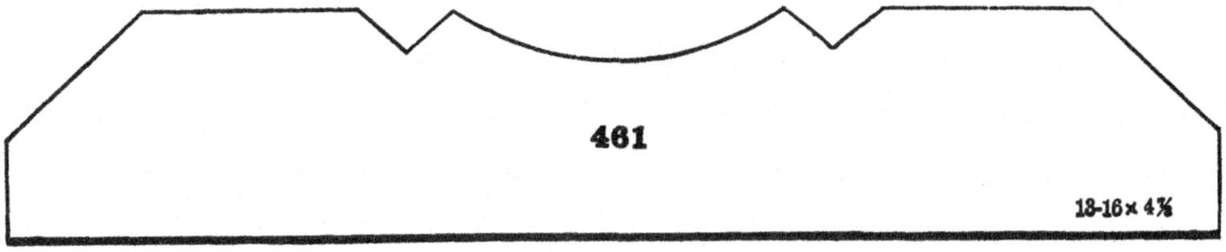
461
13-16 × 4⅝

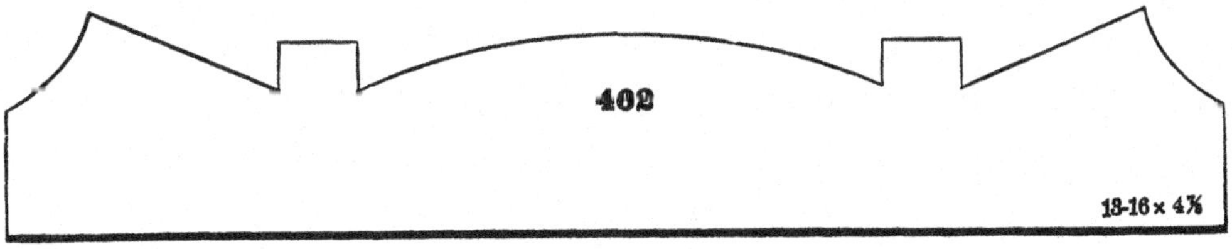
462
13-16 × 4⅝

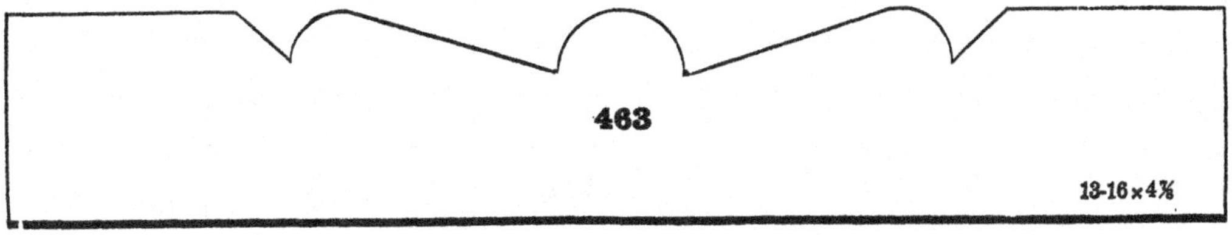
463
13-16 × 4⅝

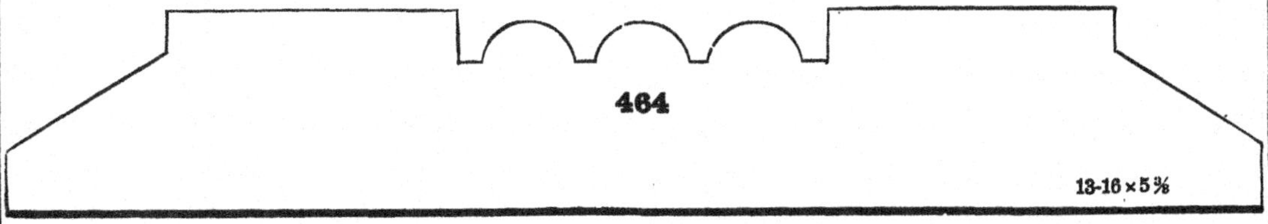
464
13-16 × 5⅜

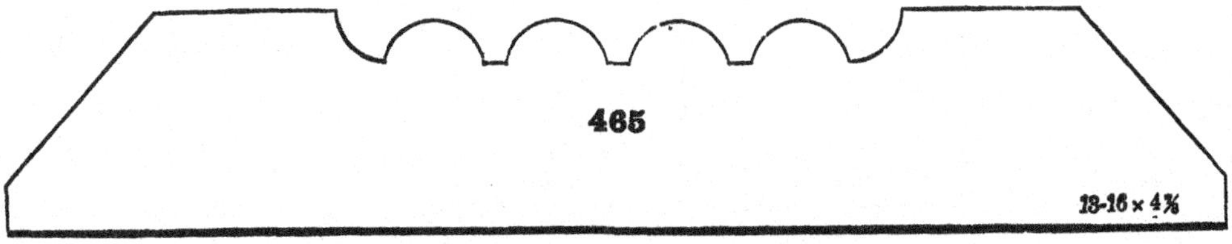
465
13-16 × 4⅝

Casings on this Page Suitable for Pilaster Finish.

EASTLAKE AND QUEEN ANNE CASINGS.

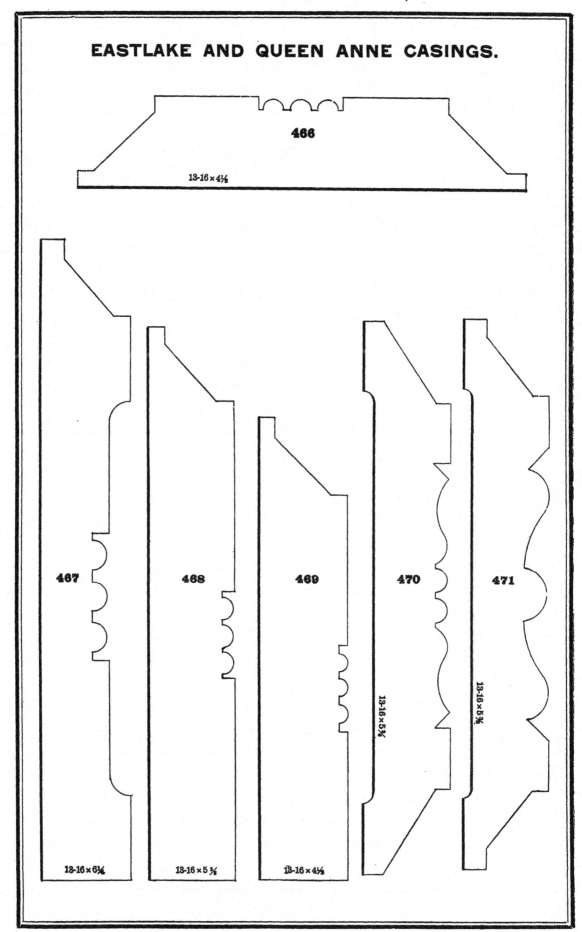

CASINGS.

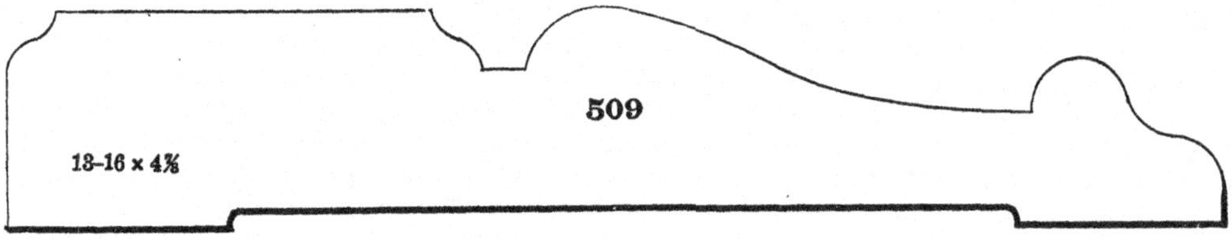
509
13-16 x 4⅝

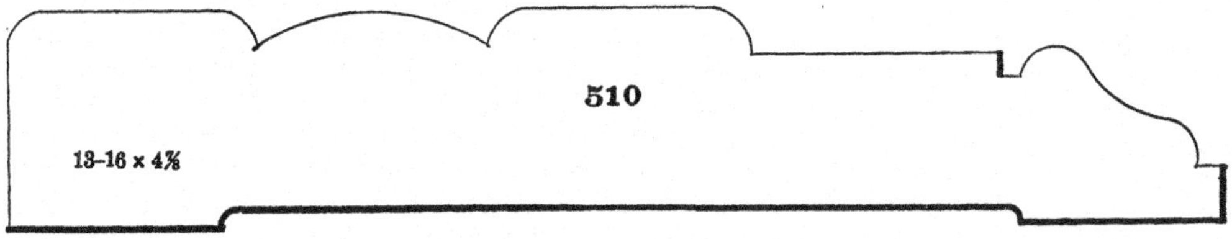
510
13-16 x 4⅝

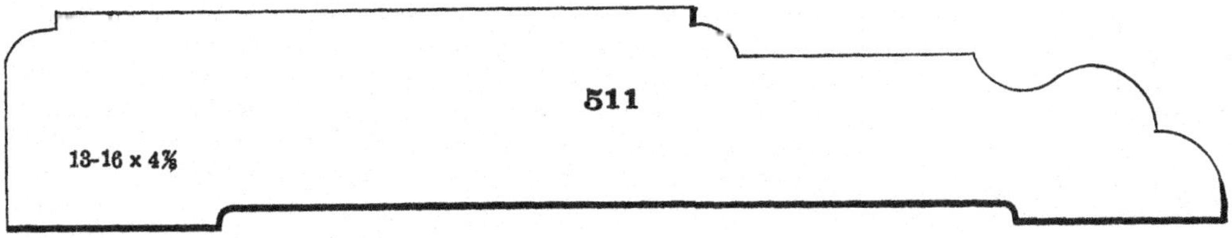
511
13-16 x 4⅝

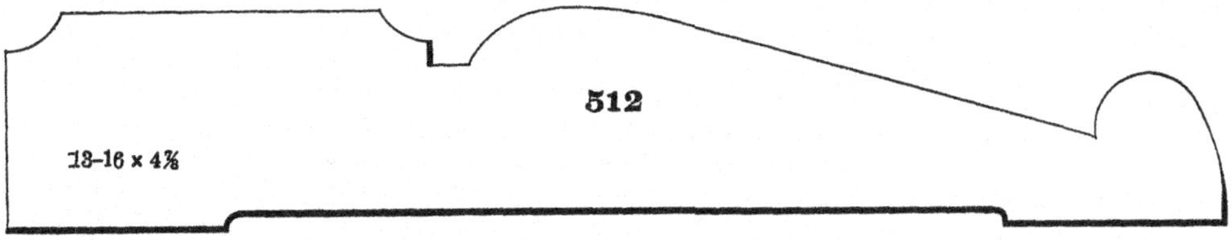
512
13-16 x 4⅝

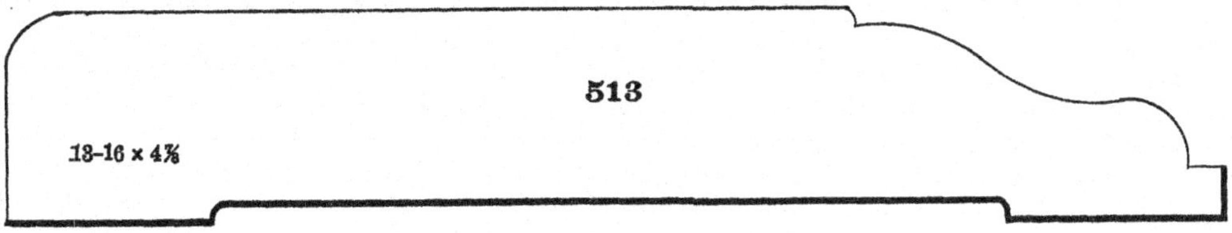
513
13-16 x 4⅝

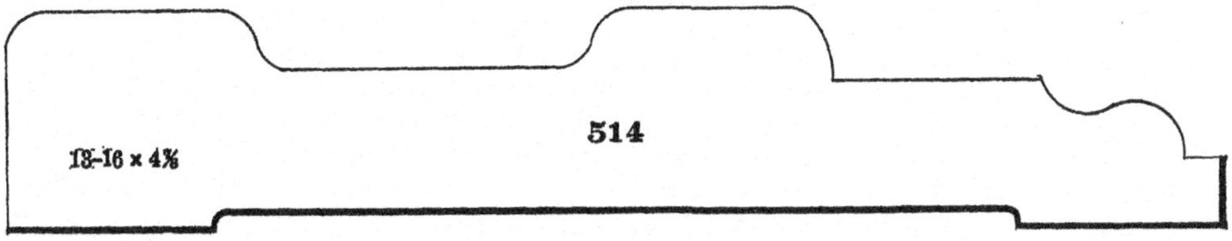
514
13-16 x 4⅝

INSIDE FINISH.

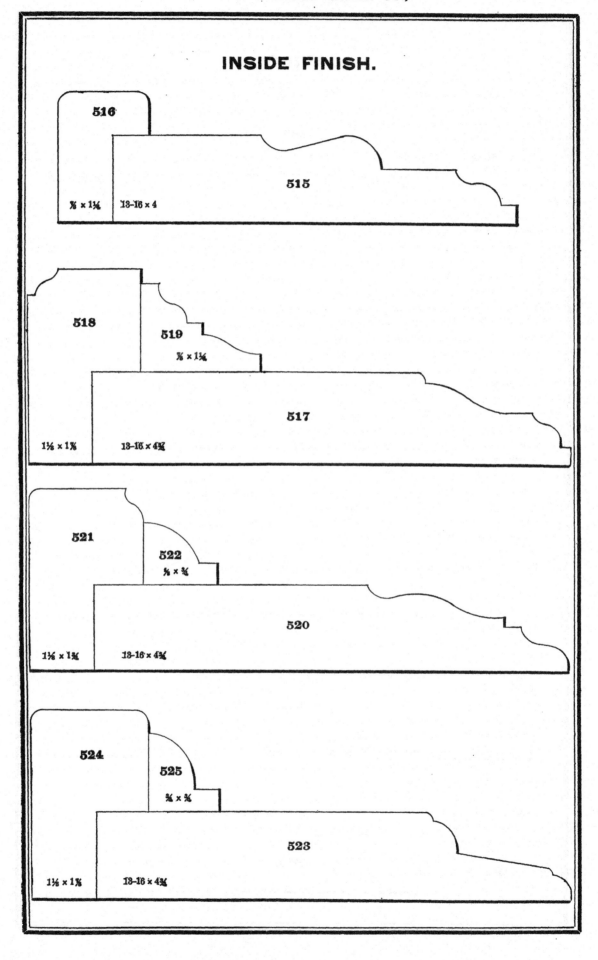

516

515

⅞ × 1¼   13–16 × 4

518

519

⅞ × 1¼

517

1⅛ × 1⅜   13–16 × 4¾

521

522

⅞ × ⅞

520

1⅛ × 1⅜   13–16 × 4¾

524

525

¾ × ¾

523

1⅛ × 1⅜   13–16 × 4¾

INSIDE FINISH.

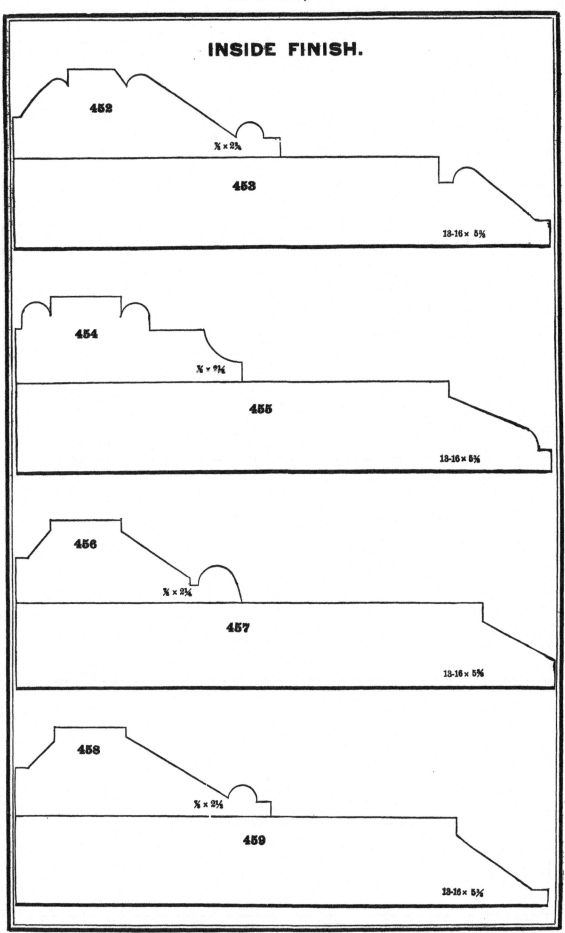

INSIDE FINISH.

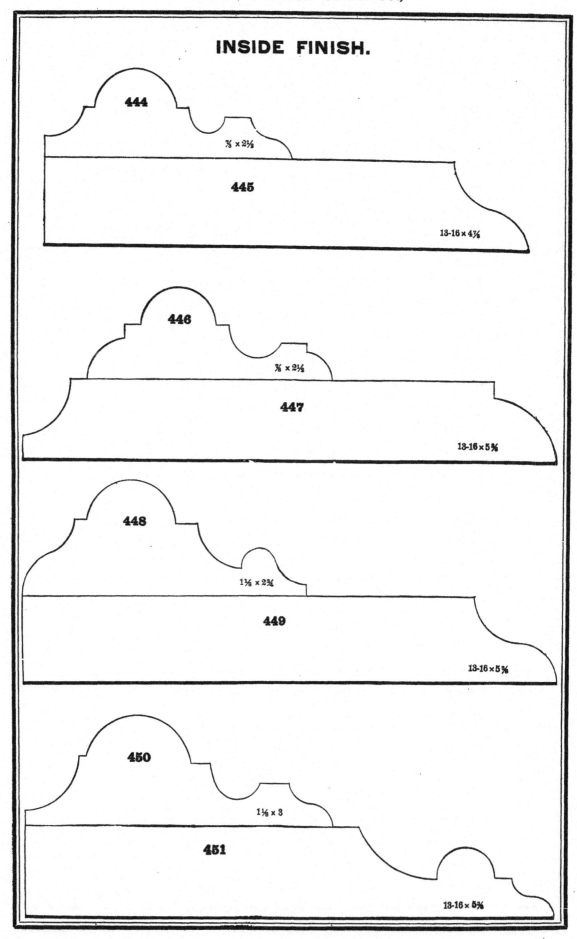

BASE.

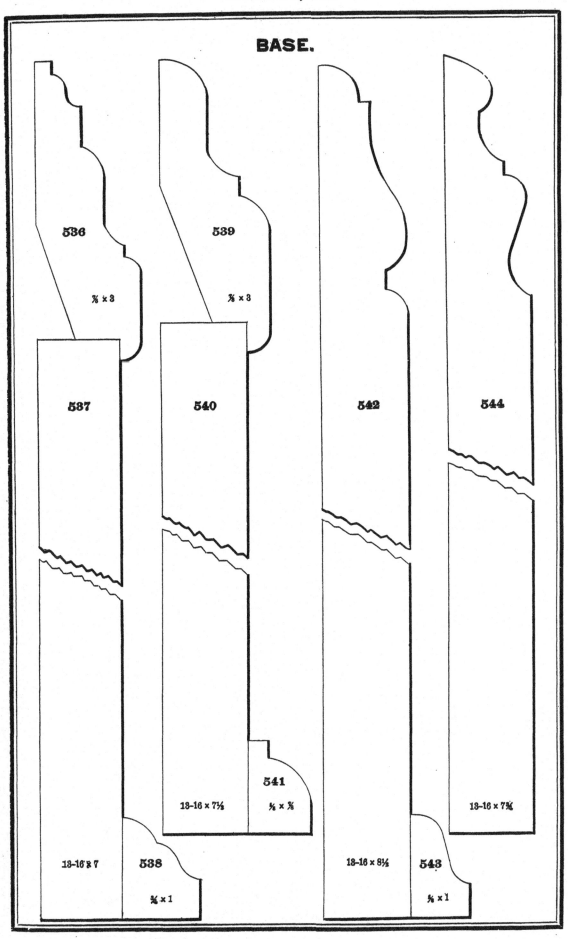

536 ⅝ × 3

539 ⅝ × 3

537

540

542

544

541 ½ × ⅝

13–16 × 7½

13–16 × 7¾

13–16 × 7

538 ¾ × 1

13–16 × 8½

543 ½ × 1

BASE.

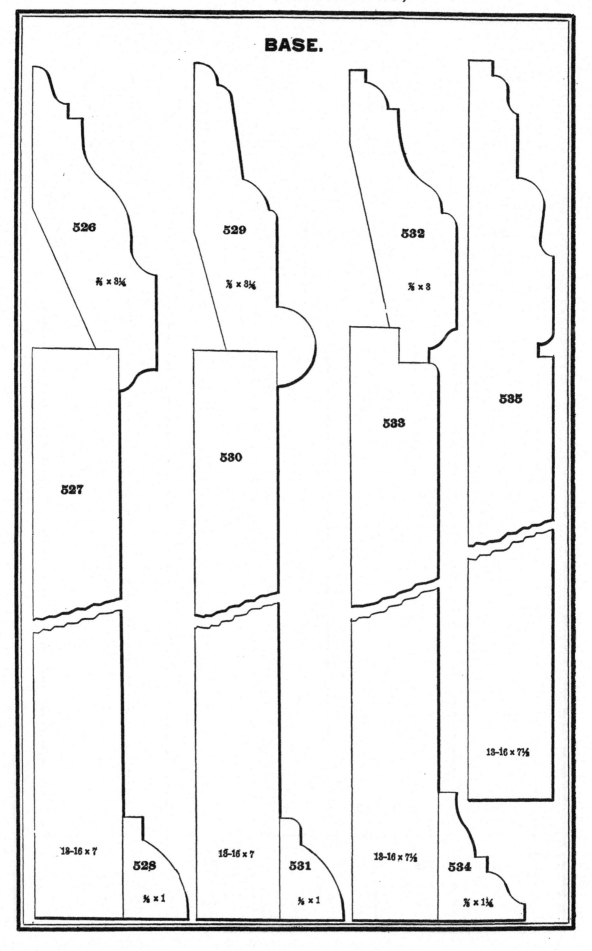

BASE.

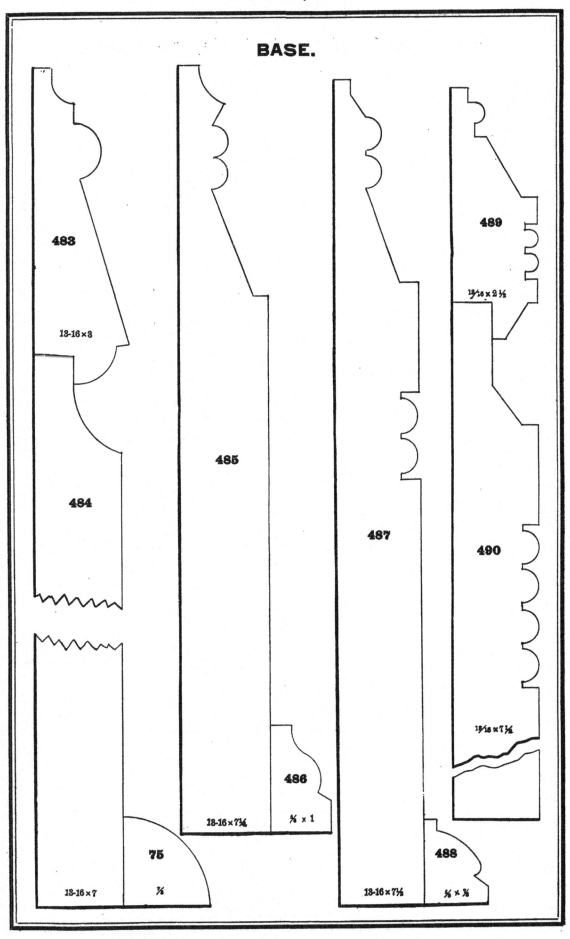

483

13-16 × 3

484

485

13-16 × 7½

486

½ × 1

75

13-16 × 7

½

487

13-16 × 7½

488

½ × ½

489

13⁄16 × 2½

490

13⁄16 × 7½

RABBETED PANEL AND BASE MOULDINGS.

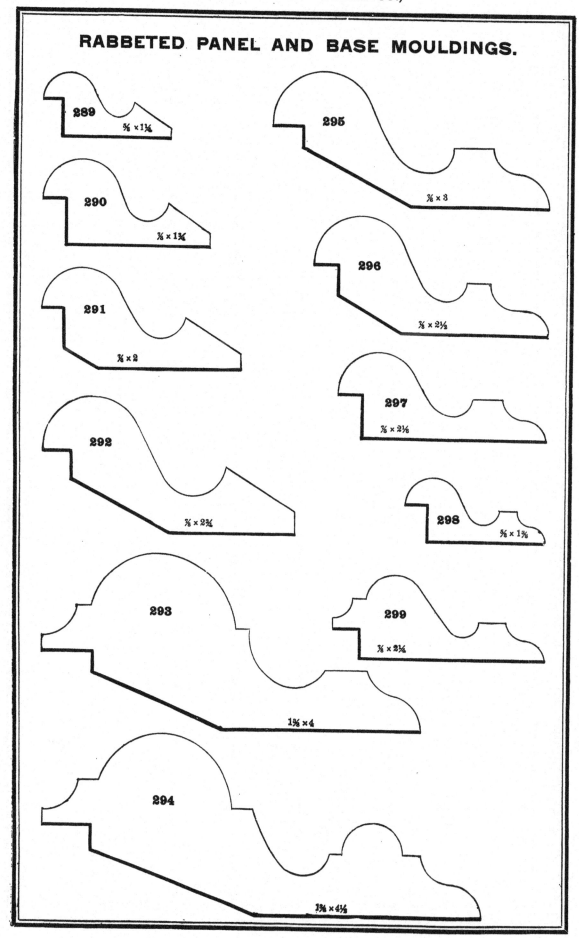

RABBETED PANEL AND BASE MOULDINGS.

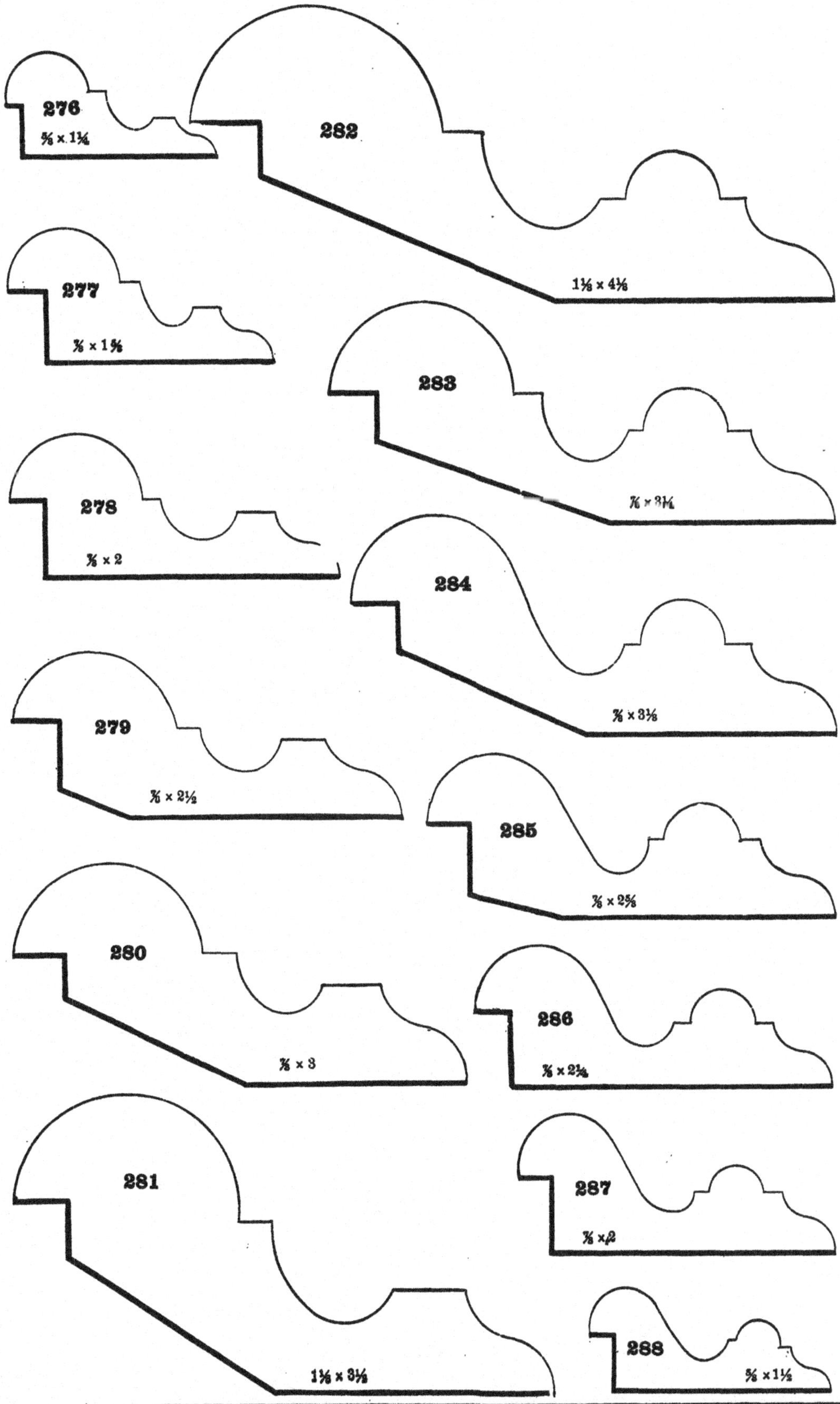
276
⅝ x 1¼
282
1⅛ x 4⅛
277
⅞ x 1⅝
283
⅞ x 3¼
278
⅝ x 2
284
⅞ x 3⅛
279
⅞ x 2½
285
⅞ x 2⅝
280
⅞ x 3
286
⅞ x 2¼
281
1⅛ x 3½
287
⅞ x 2
288
⅝ x 1½

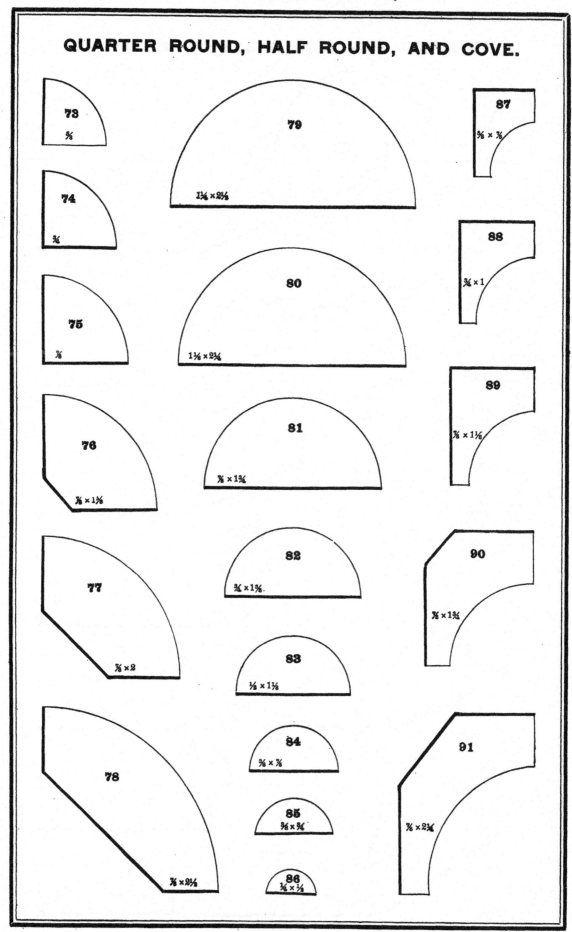

QUARTER ROUND, HALF ROUND, AND COVE.

O G STOPS.

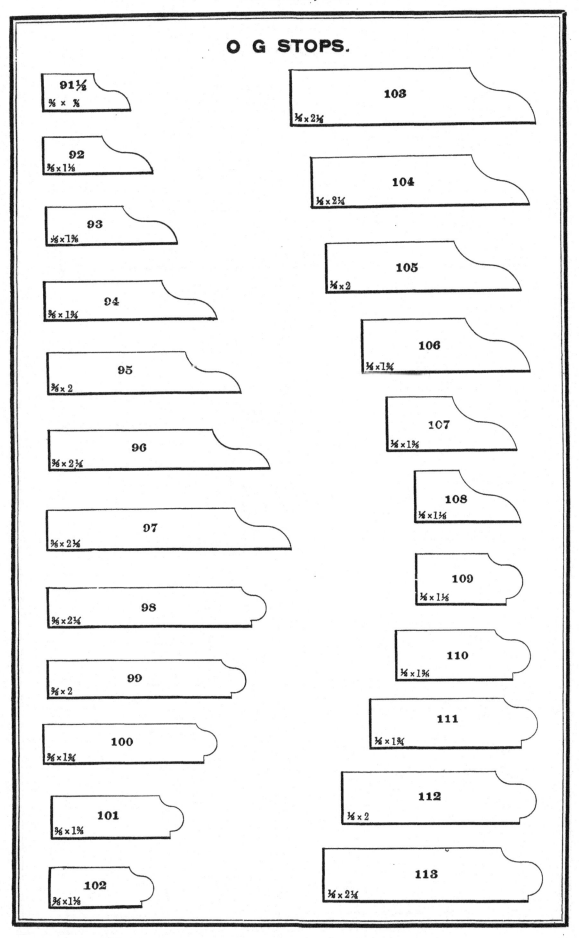

NOSINGS.

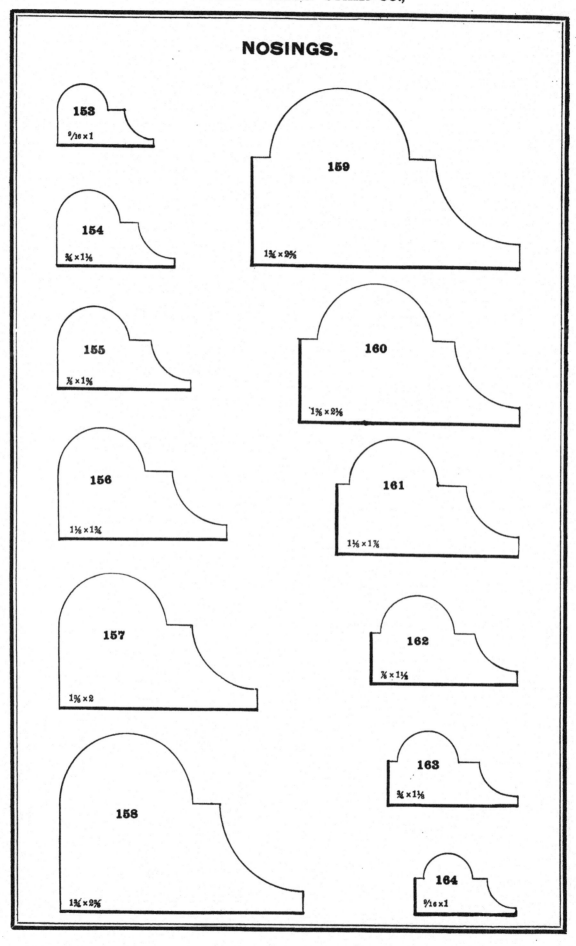

NOSINGS.

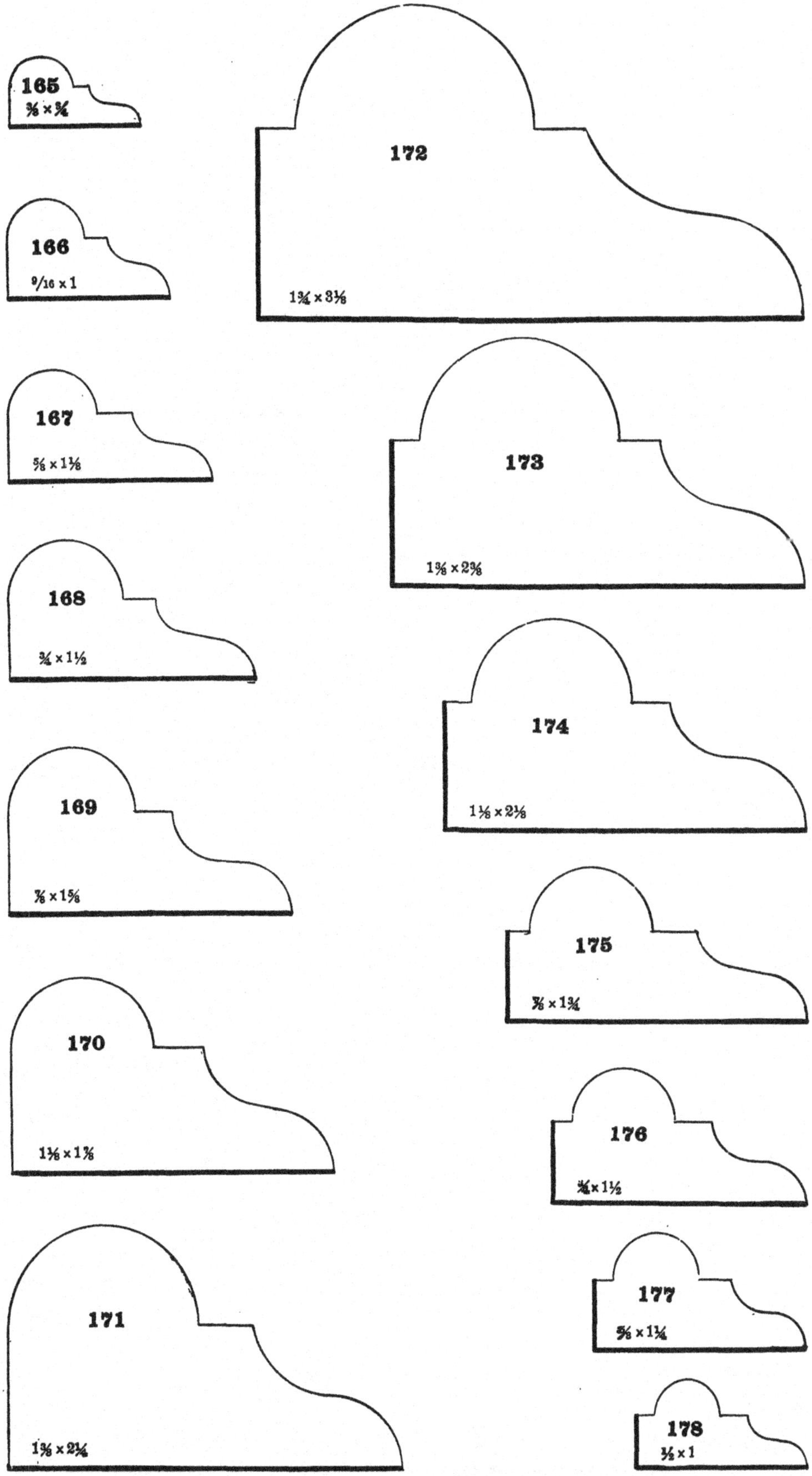
165
⅜ × ¾
166
9/16 × 1
167
⅝ × 1⅛
168
¾ × 1½
169
⅞ × 1⅝
170
1⅛ × 1⅞
171
1⅜ × 2¼
172
1¾ × 3⅛
173
1⅜ × 2⅜
174
1⅛ × 2⅛
175
⅞ × 1¾
176
¾ × 1½
177
⅝ × 1¼
178
½ × 1

NOSINGS.

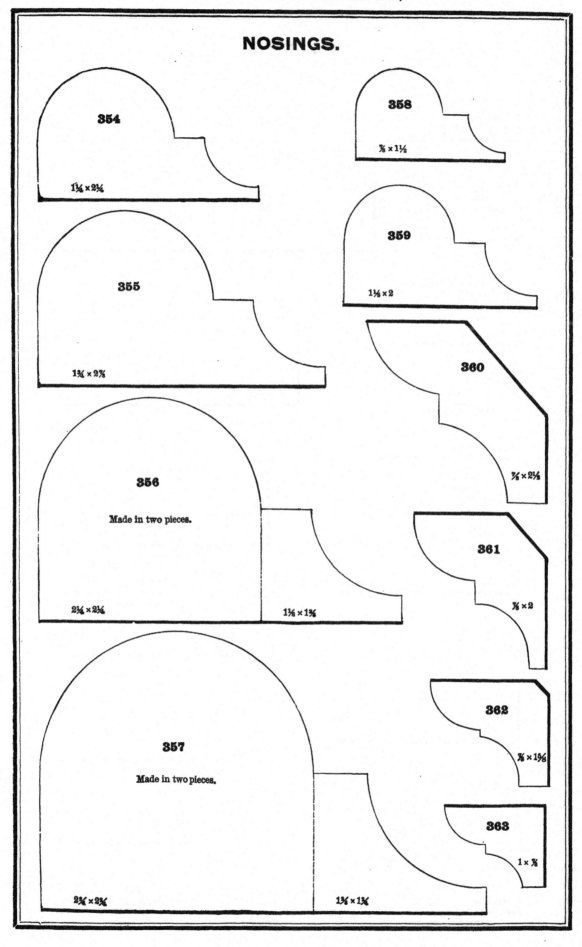

354
1¼ × 2¼

355
1¾ × 2⅝

356
Made in two pieces.
2¼ × 2¼
1⅜ × 1¾

357
Made in two pieces.
2⅜ × 2⅜
1¾ × 1¾

358
⅞ × 1½

359
1⅛ × 2

360
⅞ × 2½

361
⅞ × 2

362
⅞ × 1⅞

363
1 × ⅞

PEW BACK RAIL, WAINSCOTING CAP, AND THRESHOLDS.

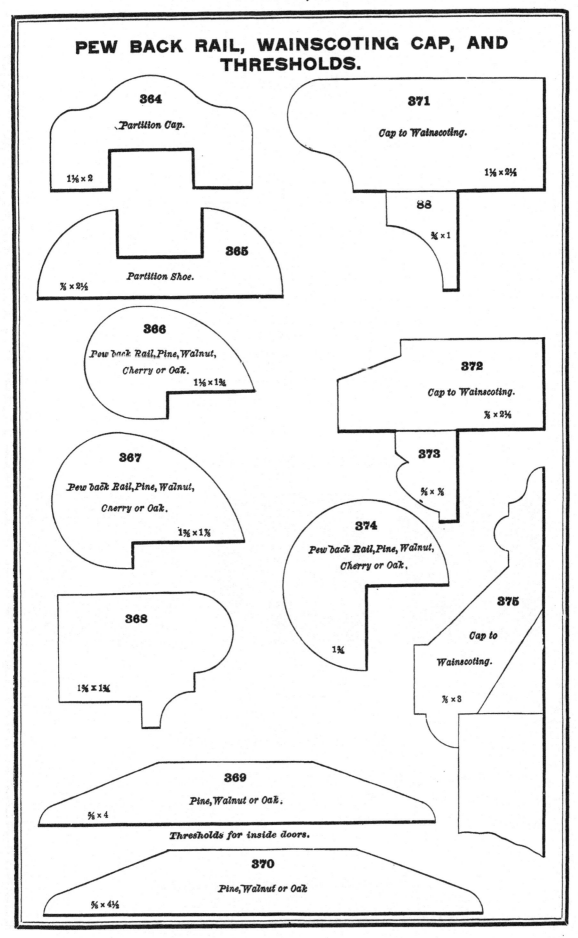

364

Partition Cap.

1⅛ x 2

371

Cap to Wainscoting.

1⅛ x 2½

88

¾ x 1

365

Partition Shoe.

⅞ x 2½

366

Pew back Rail, Pine, Walnut, Cherry or Oak.

1⅛ x 1¾

372

Cap to Wainscoting.

⅞ x 2⅛

373

⅝ x ⅞

367

Pew back Rail, Pine, Walnut, Cherry or Oak.

1⅜ x 1⅞

374

Pew back Rail, Pine, Walnut, Cherry or Oak.

1¾

368

1⅜ x 1¾

375

Cap to Wainscoting.

⅞ x 3

369

Pine, Walnut or Oak.

⅝ x 4

Thresholds for inside doors.

370

Pine, Walnut or Oak

⅝ x 4½

FLOORING.

Flooring; in any hard or soft wood.

491

CEILING.

436

Ceiling or Wainscoting,
in any hard or soft wood.

WOOD VENTILATORS.

 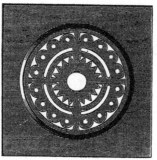 

610   **611**   **612**

INTERIOR FINISHING

Done in Maple, Ash, Red Oak, White Oak, Birch, Cherry, Sycamore, Mahogany, and all other Woods, in the best style of workmanship and of thoroughly kiln-dried material.

ESTIMATES FURNISHED IF DESIRED.

NEWEL.

6

CPSIA information can be obtained
at www.ICGtesting.com
Printed in the USA
BVOW04s2029051217

502001BV00004B/188/P